Career management via LinkedIn

Aaltje Vincent & Jacco Valkenburg

Career management via LinkedIn

Using your online network
to find new work or
challenging assignments®

Spectrum

Uitgeverij Unieboek | Het Spectrum bv, Houten-Antwerpen

Spectrum is part of Uitgeverij Unieboek | Het Spectrum bv
Postbus 97
3990 DB Houten

First published in 2010.
Originally published in Dutch by Unieboek | Het Spectrum, 2009.
Translation: Kumar Jamdagni
Cover design: De Weijer Design, Baarn
Photograph Aaltje Vincent: Marlies de Ridder
Photograph Jacco Valkenburg: Jan Vonk
Typesetting: Elgraphic bv, Schiedam

This book was written with great care. Publishing a book is a process that takes months. This
means that current changes on LinkedIn are not included in this book and that we cannot
guarantee that all information in this book is correct. For current information we would like
to refer you to: www.careermanagementvialinkedin.com

ISBN 978 90 491 0439 9
NUR 809
www.unieboekspectrum.nl
www.careermanagementvialinkedin.com

Content

Foreword

Networking, in other words, gaining personal contact with people in your professional field, is *the* way to find new work. As a business *online social network*, LinkedIn is the ideal tool for raising your profile, and building and maintaining your network. The rapid growth in the number of people placing their profiles on LinkedIn, is driving more and more companies and organizations to use LinkedIn to locate and recruit the best talent for work.

LinkedIn has many facets that make it such an exceptionally useful tool for jobseekers. But research has shown that many LinkedIn users are either not aware of the possibilities it offers, or they are not making maximum use of its potential. In this practical guide, we will take you step by step, from creating a clear profile, building and informing your network, and finding the *hiring managers* at the companies you want to work for, right till the stage of preparing you for your job interview. Once you have gone through all the steps mentioned here, you will not only begin to get a good feel of the job market and how it works, but will also develop a strong knowledge base for networking, and for applying for jobs via LinkedIn. This guide will help you ensure that:

- Your online profile, public CV and references are complete and up to date.
- You have mapped out your personal job market (i.e. where do you want to work?) using LinkedIn.
- Your contacts will find you for the work you are looking for.
- Your job interviews are well prepared, thanks to LinkedIn.

All this information is further complemented with proven tips, unique tricks and a comprehensive explanation of all the built-in tools, to make the maximum use of the possibilities offered by LinkedIn and advance your career. In our eyes, LinkedIn is the living example of the expressions: 'It's not about who you know but who knows you' and: 'Knowing who you're dealing with'.

As the authors of this guide, we aim to provide the reader with the most in-depth and up-to-date knowledge in the job-hunting sphere based on our wide and varied experience in this field. Jacco is an international recruitment expert, author of the book *Recruitment via LinkedIn,* and trains recruiters in using LinkedIn effectively. Aaltje Vincent is the author of the (Dutch) book *Jobmarketing* and is an experienced trainer helping both jobseekers and career coaches.

Our mutually complementary expertises – Jacco's as a recruiter and Aaltje's as a career coach – have proven to be indispensable in designing the structure and content of this book, making this book ideally suited to those who are already active in the job market as well as those taking a new step in their career for the first time in 20 years. It takes the LinkedIn novice by the hand, and also offers the experienced user many new insights into LinkedIn and its uses.

The result is a book that we wholeheartedly hope will provide tremendous support to your career, help you find new work or freelance assignments, and will lead to mutually successful and long-term business relationships.

We wish you lots of success in using LinkedIn to find new work and assignments!

Aaltje Vincent & Jacco Valkenburg

www.careermanagementvialinkedin.com

1. Introduction

1.1 FINDING WORK VIA LINKEDIN

Finding work via LinkedIn is becoming increasingly common. This leads to two very important and interesting questions: 'How can you use LinkedIn effectively to find work? And how do recruiters use LinkedIn?'

Of all the 'social networking sites' that exist, such as Facebook and Twitter, LinkedIn is the only one that is considered to be for professionals, and is therefore also considered to be the most reliable. More than 60 million people have created a LinkedIn profile. At its most basic, a typical LinkedIn profile consists of the user's curriculum vitae, and the contacts he/she has chosen to connect with. The power of creating such a profile lies in the fact that users determine their own 'work profile', which can be viewed at all times, not just by their own network, but also by employers, potential clients and recruiters.

The extremely rapid growth of LinkedIn has been fuelled by the trends in today's job market. Take for example Karin Winters, aged 47. She found a job via LinkedIn. Winters, who was teaching at the time, wrote in her update displayed directly above her LinkedIn profile: 'I am looking for a new challenge.' 'Within a week I received three serious job offers.' For her current employer, Paragin, it was the first time they had filled a job vacancy via LinkedIn. A colleague at Paragin was a member of Winters' network and saw her request. Her job experience matched the newly vacant position and, after a positive interview, she started work at Paragin.

Organizations prefer to fill their vacancies via the personal networks of their own staff. Experience shows that new employees recruited via an organization's own personnel are also more productive and more satisfied in their job! Employer market research confirms this; the majority of vacancies are being filled via the contacts of a company's own staff. Additionally, companies prefer to approach potential candidates directly – which is an effective and inexpensive way to recruit. So 'hiring managers' and recruiters embrace LinkedIn as a unique database of potential candidates for all types of vacancies. Furthermore, for jobseekers it is a fantastic way of 'putting yourself in the spotlight' for new work.

TIP: LinkedIn consists of many elements. We will take you through all its possibilities step by step. For an overview of all the different elements, see 'LinkedIn basics' on page 116.

1.2 WHOOZY?

Recruiters[1] are keen to obtain as much information about candidates as possible before hiring them as their new colleague. In order to screen candidates, recruiters make use of various search engines and online profile sites. They make particular use of specialized (vertical) search engines that gather a lot of personal information, and present this in an orderly way. A vertical search engine searches on a specific subject (your name, for example) more thoroughly than search engines like Google or Yahoo.

Whoozy.com is one such vertical search engine which searches all kinds of resources that can provide personal information about individuals. All this information is displayed in one place to make it easier to analyse. By using intelligent search technology, information about one person can be filtered from different databases, such as Twitter, Facebook, Classmates, Google, Yahoo, YouTube and LinkedIn. You can then view the specific source, for example Twitter or LinkedIn. In this way, a recruiter gets a

---

1. Recruiters are people who recruit new personnel: human resource managers, the management or consultants of intermediaries such as temping agencies, or secondment- and recruitment and selection agencies.

broad perspective on the potential candidate; this could be information about the candidate from the past or his/her up-to-date LinkedIn profile!

It is good to take into account that recruiters all work with search engines. With LinkedIn, the user fully controls the way his/her *work* experience is presented. And this is why recruiters consider LinkedIn as extremely reliable.

 TIP: Initiate a search on your own name on the site www.whoozy.com or 123people.com, and see for yourself what traces your own name leaves on the internet.

1.3   PERSONAL BRANDING AND KNOWING WHAT YOU WANT

Personal branding is a concept that is becoming increasingly widespread. Personal branding means that you take time to reflect on the 'image' you evoke when others see you, and what they think about you afterwards. You actively try to portray an image of yourself that you would like others, such as recruiters, to have. An image that makes you unique and makes you stand out from the rest. This means that you think about your personal and professional goals in life and reflect on whether and how you are communicating these on Twitter or Facebook, or on LinkedIn. Personal branding therefore starts with self-knowledge and self-analysis.

What is your passion? And what do you hate? Self-analysis can help here. It is all about building a strong 'personal' image that ensures you are associated with the right things, which will eventually get you closer to your goals, such as a new job or assignment. It has to be absolutely clear who you are and what you stand for. And you will need to consider your choices carefully regarding how you want to communicate this, and what other people see of you through these sites. It is very easy to leave a trail on Twitter, Facebook and LinkedIn, so be extremely aware of this. In very simple terms, your image consists of making your strong points even stronger and always acting in line with them, in a way that makes you stand out from the crowd. Because you need to stand out. Be aware of what you want; whether you are a job applicant or a freelancer, there are many other candidates or rivals out there.

When you are applying for jobs via LinkedIn, it is crucial to know exactly where your talents lie and which added value you can provide. What solution can you provide to which problem? Translating this into a position or positions, in a branch or branches that are relevant for you is an excellent starting point.

To help you get a clear picture of your talents and ambitions, there are lots of self-help books you can read and tests you can do, or you can seek the guidance of a career counsellor. Another good strategy is to talk to people who know you well – good friends, but also and especially people in your work environment – and to ask them for advice (what work do they see you doing and why?). Once you have a clear idea of what work you would like to be seen as doing, described in terms of the position or positions you are looking for, this will be the most effective starting point for your profile on LinkedIn. If you use LinkedIn the right way, it will help you create a *buzz* about yourself, which can result in opportunities and possibilities that you would otherwise not have had (see also chapter 5 on networking).

Summing up then: to get that new job or assignment that you are looking for, the way you are 'recognized' on LinkedIn is very important. Take control yourself. This book will guide you step by step!

1.4 THE ROUTE OF THE JOB VACANCY

Job vacancies[2] arise every day, particularly with job mobility being high. Employers try to fill a vacancy with the right candidate as quickly and as cheaply as possible. The route of a job vacancy may be a long one; in general, it takes a few weeks before a vacancy is made known to the outside world.

---

2. Note for freelancers: wherever you see the term 'job vacancy' or 'vacancy', you can also interpret this as: 'an assignment'.

Those who have found a new job or assignment elsewhere are the first ones to know about a new job vacancy. For example, John Doe is currently working as a PR- and communication officer for a museum in Washington. He applies for a job at a museum in New York and on Friday, late afternoon he hears he has got the job! He is the first to know that there is now a job vacancy in Washington; a job vacancy 'has been born' due to him leaving that job. Those who hear about his resignation soon after – and therefore of the brand new vacancy – are people in his immediate circle of friends, family, fellow sports club members, or, for example, his book club. On Monday morning he hands in his notice to his manager and announces his departure in the weekly meeting. The news spreads through the whole organization like wildfire, the other teams, the other departments all hear about it, via e-mails, text messages and Twitter. All these colleagues talk about it at home that evening, they inform their friends, and so the news spreads further.

1.4.1 Informal networking
The example above involves what we call a 'replacement vacancy': someone leaves and someone else is hired in replacement. What often happens in such cases is that people within the company say: 'Does anyone know someone who could fill this vacancy?' Or: 'I know someone for the job.'

Let's now imagine the owner of a small company on his Saturday morning run in a flash of inspiration thinks: 'I want to have all the figures available at any time, I will employ a bookkeeper.' This is what we call an 'additional vacancy'. The next step is: 'Who knows someone who can fill this vacancy?' The owner then talks to people at his hockey club on Saturday afternoon, and on Saturday evening he sees a couple of good friends and asks them: 'Do you know a good bookkeeper?'

People who are *now* doing the job that you're after, are the first to hear when they need a new colleague.

Very often, more than a hundred people will have been made aware of the vacancy within a few days by mere word-of-mouth. Labour market studies consistently show that three out of four vacancies are filled through networking. Seventy percent of the vacancies are filled through so-called informal contacts.[3]

In this phase, LinkedIn is of immeasurable value. Colleagues can now say: 'This job is ideal for John Doe, just take a look at his LinkedIn profile.'

Sometimes companies work with 'referral programmes', rewarding employees who introduce good candidates; see page 63. Research also shows that employees who are recruited through informal contacts are more satisfied with their job posting (source: *Angami White Paper*, 2000).

1.4.2 Own website
Then the vacancy appears on the website of the company or organization. This is where the vacancy can be publicly viewed for the first time. It can take weeks before it gets to this stage. There are a number of reasons for this. Firstly, an employer prefers to fill the vacancy informally. Secondly, someone has to create the text for the job vacancy, which then has to be approved by the hiring manager, the HR department, and sometimes the webmaster. Only then is the vacancy ready to be published. Initially it may only appear on the intranet for a few days or even weeks, and then made visible for everyone outside the organization via internet.

1.4.3 Intermediaries
If no suitable candidates can be found informally, or if responses to the website do not produce any leads, then a company or organization can hire an intermediary to help with the recruitment.
For example:

- temporary job agencies
- recruitment and selection agencies
- secondment agencies

These agencies also search profiles on LinkedIn to find suitable candidates.

---

3. Source: UWV Werkbedrijf, *Job application tips for the over-45s.*

1.4.4 Newspaper and jobsites/job boards

A company or organization will typically wait a few weeks before deciding to place a job advertisement. This can be done in the following ways:

- In a trade journal, a trade newspaper, or on the website of the branch association (for example of the housing corporation) or the professional association (for example of accountants)
- Via a job advertisement in the newspaper (national, local)
- Via generic job vacancy sites/job boards, for example Monster or Careerbuilder

At this moment, with the vacancy already a few weeks old, the people who will respond are those who are nevertheless hearing about the vacancy for the first time and find the job appealing. For thousands of people, it will be a new vacancy, and they will respond in high numbers!

The lesson is clear: if you want to maximise your chances of finding a new job, you will need to get to know the people who are now doing the work you would like to do. So that these people will know where to find you when they are looking for a new colleague!

1.5 LOOKING FOR WORK FOR THE OVER-45S

For people above the age of 45, looking for a job via the newspaper or websites is rather difficult. At the moment, the labour market operates in such a way that written job applications from over-45s do not easily lead to job interviews. Labour market studies have shown that people over 45 typically find new work via their own networks; they are no longer an interesting segment for job advertisers. People above 45 therefore, need their own 'ambassadors'. These can be recruited via:

- one's own network, for which LinkedIn is an effective tool
- one of the intermediaries, such as a temporary employment agency, a recruitment and selection agency, or a secondment- or interim management agency; these agencies are also active on LinkedIn

2. Online social networks

2.1 THE RECRUITER FOLLOWS THE CANDIDATE

In the past, companies placed job advertisements in the daily newspapers because everyone read them. Since the end of the 1990s, jobsites (job boards) have slowly, but surely, been replacing newspaper job advertisements for almost all target groups. Jobsites are extremely efficient in bringing supply and demand together. Through these sites, active jobseekers can be reached by companies more quickly and cheaper.

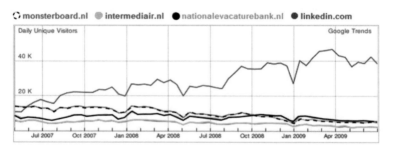

SOURCE: GOOGLE TRENDS, MAY 2009

Currently, online social networks are being used on a massive scale. In some countries, like the Netherlands, more than 80% of all professionals have a profile on one of the many online social networks such as Hyves, Facebook and LinkedIn. Amongst the top 20 of the most visited websites in the Netherlands, you will find a number of social media platforms such as Facebook, Wikipedia and MSN alongside search engines, banks and news (in fact these social media platforms are all in the top 10). It is therefore hardly surprising that recruiters and human resource managers have discovered these social media as a recruitment channel. After all, recruiters and human resource managers follow their target group of potential candidates in order to reach them most effectively, just like marketeers do. On the one hand, companies use these social media as an advertising channel by placing jobs (paid or free), banners and advertisements. On the other hand, these media are increasingly and successfully used as free public CV databases, where individuals looking for new jobs can post their professional information and interests. This latter aspect particularly is creating a minor revolution in companies. Whereas previously the recruitment and selection agencies employed personnel and resources to build up a unique and valuable CV database, this exercise has nowadays become almost totally redundant. Why should you invest a lot of time and money in building up a huge CV database, if all up-to-date profile information can be found on the internet?

Profiles also have the advantage of providing much more information than just a chronological summary of employers and work experience. Online profiles contain supplementary and up-to-date information such as photos, personal and professional networks, interests and recommendations. Online profiles also function as a person's business card, and are usually personalized with colours and photos in the background in so far as the features of the social platform allow such possibilities. From escapades over the weekend, professional blog articles, messages between friends to holiday snaps. You can read all about what a person is doing at the moment. It is good to be aware of the fact that (almost) everything you place on the internet is public and can therefore be found, as we explained in the section 'Whoozy?' (page 12).

You can view this development as a danger, but it also offers opportunities. For instance, you can use these social media in your personal branding strategy. In the past, all you had was a traditional CV to help you secure an interview with a potential employer or client. Now it is possible to use an online business profile, such as on LinkedIn, to be found, and it allows you to provide much more information. LinkedIn offers, for example, the possibility of placing blog articles, videos or PowerPoint presentations in your profile. In other words, many more possibilities of presenting yourself as an expert in a certain field, or, to put it more accurately, as the solution to a company's problem! And this applies to both jobseekers and freelancers.

2.2 THE RISE OF ONLINE SOCIAL NETWORKS

Online social networks are not new. The first forms of online communities date as far back as 1985 (The WELL). Classmates.com dates back to 1995. With the advent of Friendster, MySpace and Bebo between 2002 and 2004, we were introduced to the type of online social networks that we are familiar with today, with the functionality of creating profiles and sending messages to other users. The breakthrough was reached in 2007, when online social networks such as MySpace (launched in August 2003) and the international network LinkedIn (May 2003) were embraced with open arms.

Nowadays there are hundreds and thousands of social websites in all kinds of categories, such as:

- Business networks: LinkedIn, Plaxo, Xing, etc.
- Friends' networks: Facebook, MySpace, Classmates, Netlog
- Niche networks: Bookmootch (books), Couchsurfing (travel), BarackObama.com and Last.fm (music).
- Video/photo/slide networks: YouTube (video), Flickr (photo), Slideshare (slide shows)
- Mobile phone networks: AirG and Jumbuck in regions such as Africa and Australia
- Private networks: groups that only work via invitations such as Ormit (alumni network) and aSmallWorld (for the jet set and elite)

2.3 THE POWER OF ONLINE NETWORKS

The process you go through to find new work or a new freelance assignment has various aspects and steps, the most important of which are creating and building a profile, and maintaining your personal relations network. Online networks are extremely useful tools in all phases of the job application process. They can help you with finding a job vacancy (whether it has been made public or not), obtaining a job interview, and getting an idea of a suitable salary range for your skills and work. The following are some of the most important reasons for using online networks to find new work:

- Finding job vacancies (whether they have been made public or not)
- Personal branding; being found by recruiters with suitable vacancies or assignments
- Building a network with companies and individuals that could be useful in developing your career
- Maintaining a permanent address book with up-to-date data
- Collecting information related to your career, your personal job market, area of specialization, etc
- Having access to an online communication platform that is available 24 hours a day (as a supplement to e-mail and telephone)

LinkedIn also contributes towards enhancing your visibility on the internet. This is thanks to LinkedIn's high Google PageRank. PageRank is a method of classifying pages on the internet according to their importance. The LinkedIn website and the profiles on it have a high relevance and value in Google PageRank, with the result that if people search your name in Google, your LinkedIn profile scores high in the search results (often in the top ten search results displayed).

Thus there are plenty of reasons to study LinkedIn more closely! In this book, we will take you through all the possibilities LinkedIn has for finding new work, step by step. And you will get unique tips on how to use the options LinkedIn offers.

2.4 FACTS AND FIGURES ON LINKEDIN
One of the success factors of LinkedIn has been that, right from the start, many prominent and important world citizens have had their profile on LinkedIn. In the first years these were influential investors from Silicon Valley, later, celebrities like Bill Gates, Hillary Clinton and Barack Obama also joined the network. LinkedIn has since grown to become one of the most popular online social networks in the world.

What makes LinkedIn so unique is that it particularly focuses on business networking, and is an outstanding mix of people from all kinds of industries. Many big companies structurally recruit new personnel via LinkedIn. And that fact alone says it all really.

The following is an overview of LinkedIn in figures obtained from various internet sources:

1. LinkedIn has been running since 5 May 2003; its head office is located in Mountain View (California). There are sales offices in Chicago, Omaha, New York, London, Sydney, Mumbai and Amsterdam.
2. There are 65 million user profiles worldwide. 42% of the users are from the US, followed by 14% from India, 7% from Great Britain and 3.6% from the Netherlands.
3. Every twelve days, more than a million new profiles are created.
4. The profiles of these LinkedIn users indicate that they are experienced (an average of fifteen years of work experience), and are often in decision-making roles in companies or organizations.
5. 80% of the members are between the ages of 24 and 54.
6. The average LinkedIn user is 43 years old, has fifteen years of work experience and earns more than 107,000 dollars a year.
7. LinkedIn users have an average of sixty connections and spend twenty minutes a week on LinkedIn.
8. A million management team members have their profile on LinkedIn, including CEOs of all the *Fortune 500* companies.
9. A total of more than 600,000 'groups' are created.

3. How do recruiters work?

Jacco Valkenburg, co-author of this book, has been working as an external consultant for global recruitment and talent management solutions since 1996. In this chapter he describes the way in which recruiters from big and small companies proceed with filling job vacancies and temporary assignments, freelance or otherwise.

According to a study conducted in 2006, companies use an average of 1.87 recruitment channels when looking for new personnel. This is not much when you consider the various ways that exist for communicating job vacancies and recruiting new personnel. Examples of these include:

- Print advertisements

- Online advertising

- Outdoor advertising (billboards, buses)
- Direct marketing via (e-)mail and RSS
- SMS marketing

- Open job application
- Temporary job agencies, recruitment and selection agencies
- Employee referrals

- Recruitment PR and communication
- CV databases and searching via internet
- Internal recruitment
- Recruitment of ex-employees
- Recruitment of interns and students
- Guerrilla- and viral marketing campaigns
- Job boards (generic and niche)
- Direct approaches/headhunting
- Social networks (LinkedIn, Twitter, Facebook)

- Search engine marketing and optimization
- Competitions and business games

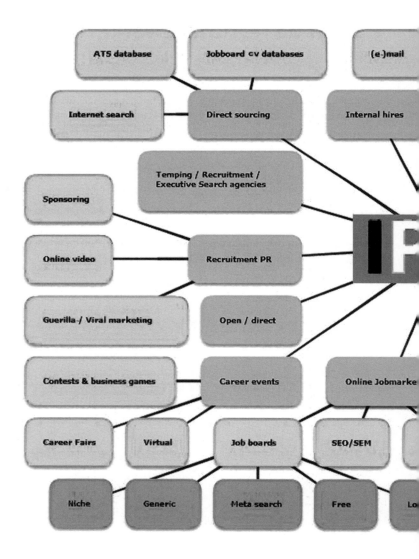

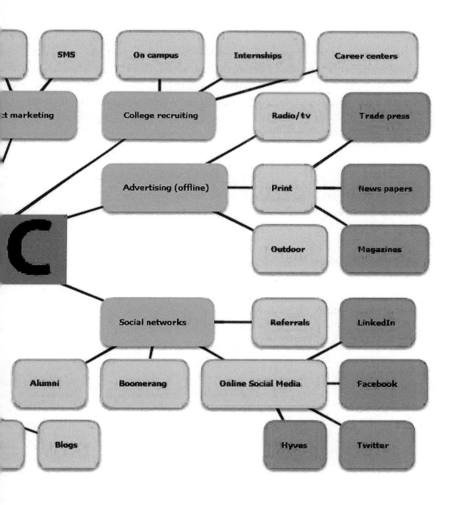

- (Online) career events
- Sponsoring and seminars

- Own career site
- New media (blogs, YouTube)

The ways in which companies organize their recruitment and selection processes vary enormously. Companies in which recruitment and selection is performed by the hiring managers themselves – these are often smaller companies – vary tremendously from companies that approach recruitment in a professional and more strategic context, and that have a separate department and/or officer specially for recruitment. For each type of vacancy, a different recruitment channel is used, the channel that is appropriate for that vacancy!

The most effective recruitment channels, according to a Dutch study in 2008[4] are summarized below according to the 'lifecycle' of the job vacancy (page 14).

Informal recruiting (people who work or have worked at the recruiting firm already know you or they can put you forward via inside information):
Friends and acquaintances/network 20%
Internal vacancies 5%
Visiting or calling a company 5%
Outplacement company 4%
Via internships 3%
Via career centres 3%
Via school 2%
Advertisement in a shop or shop window 1%
Other 8%
Total 51%

Via own company site:
Company site 2%
Open job application 8%
Total 10%

4. Source: *Arbeidsmarkt Gedrag Onderzoek* (*Labour Market Behaviour Study*) 2007-2008 (n = 32.564)

Via intermediaries:
Temporary employment agencies 13%
Recruitment and selection agencies 3%
Headhunters 2%
Total 18%

Via advertising:
Job site 10%
Newspaper 6%
(Free) local weekly paper 4%
E-mail service (job agent) 2%
Trade journal or magazine 1%
Total 23%

The recruiter, working on behalf of companies or intermediaries, follows the candidate. This means that the expected trend in recruiting is that online channels will make it increasingly possible for the recruiters to find you, instead of you having to find the job. So your online profile will become crucial for you. Additionally, you will need to resort to it more often if you want to find new work. The times of *lifelong employment* are behind us. People will fulfil a position for increasingly short periods; an average time span of two years is no longer exceptional. Your profile, keeping it up-to-date, and networking are what it is all about now, and so it will be for the rest of your working life.

3.1 HIRING MANAGERS

For all, the employed, jobseekers, interim managers and freelancers, it is of crucial importance to build up good (network) relationships with the decision-makers in the industry, or in other words the 'end users': the managers of a department. These hiring managers may be willing to engage in an orientation meeting and provide useful career tips and advice. Many companies that are interested in recruiting fresh graduates even offer this as a standard service, from open days with workshops to individual breakfast sessions. Make use of them!

It is also good to realize that temporary positions or assignments are often not handled by the HRM department. Mostly the managers themselves are responsible for hiring external staff. In big organizations where many external employees are hired, dedicated (purchasing) departments are in place. The role of the human resource manager will, in these cases, often be limited to purely administrative support. So this is an extra reason for freelancers to build and maintain a good relationship with both current and former managers.

Few business managers are involved in recruitment and selection of personnel on a daily basis. In terms of recruitment, they typically operate in a traditional way. This means that managers usually do what do they always have done and use traditional media such as print, job boards (job vacancy databases on the internet) and agencies to advertise their vacancies.

In certain sectors (for example, the healthcare- and government sectors), relatively more use is made of print media such as newspapers and magazines. But this approach may change rapidly in the coming years when business managers will embrace social media more and more. They too will get used to maintaining a professional online network for recruitment purposes. Furthermore, due to the fact that most vacancies are filled via personal relations, it is well worth keeping in touch with managers if you are looking for a new career move or interim assignment, either actively or passively.

3.2 CORPORATE RECRUITERS AND HRM STAFF

In medium- and large-sized companies, HRM staff and managers play key roles in the recruitment and selection procedure. They are not only responsible for approving a job advertisement, but are also involved in the choice of the recruitment channels, monitoring the quality of incoming personnel, and completing the administrative or logistical procedures.

Organizations that have set up their own professional recruitment department use on average seven different recruitment methods .These departments use fewer external recruitment and selection agencies because they are internally equipped to use new ways of finding talent in addition to the existing job boards and print advertisements. These departments are involved in a transition process from an ad hoc reactive manner of recruitment (advertising), to a strategic and proactive approach, focussed on long-term and good relations (social networks). Organizations that consider recruitment a professional activity, work on long-term relationships with their applicants. They try – even before you have applied – to connect with you, via for example talent pools and groups on LinkedIn. In this way, they are able to respond more quickly and more efficiently to your job application!

Today, many (big) organizations have automated their recruitment and selection procedures. The only way to respond to vacancies at these companies is online. A hand-written letter or a CV by post will stand out, but not for the better. Recruitment processes are currently no longer adapted to dealing with these. Although it is occasionally tiresome to fill in one or several online forms, modern-day recruitment systems offer many benefits to jobseekers (depending on the software):

1. All recruiters or personnel officers in the company can find your CV in the database that has been built up.
2. Applying for other positions is made easy.
3. You can keep your profile or CV up-to-date online.
4. You have total control over information. You can remove data yourself, or make it inactive.
5. The application process can be tracked both by you and by recruiters.
6. You can make use of a so-called job agent; in other words you will be the first to get an alert by e-mail when an appropriate position in the company becomes available.
7. Contact information and the vacancy you had applied for remain visible, even after the vacancy has been filled.

As soon as you have charted your personal labour market and the potential employers you are looking to work with, you can start building a long-term relationship. You can do this in a variety of ways. You can contact the HRM or recruitment department and decision-makers and managers in the organization, and you can make use of 'job agents' or RSS feeds to keep up-to-date with new relevant vacancies or freelance assignments. Search engines such as Google Alerts and Indeed can also help you through their automated searches on the internet for new vacancies. The techniques for achieving this via LinkedIn will be described later on in this book.

3.3 JOB BOARDS

The importance of job boards, where vacancies can be placed if paid for and CVs can be viewed – again if paid for – will continue to exist in the short term despite the success of online social networks, though the form and the profit strategy are likely to change significantly. It is therefore still important to ensure that you can easily be found on job boards. A lot of advice that you will find in this book regarding your profile on LinkedIn, is also applicable for placing your CV on a job board.

To optimize this process, here are some additional tips to keep in mind specifically when operating on job boards:

1. Update your CV at regular intervals so that you appear at the top of the search results. Recruiters can see when you last modified your profile. This is a sign that you are still active in the job market. Just changing a full stop or comma in the text is often enough. But do not overdo it for you may come across as desperate; so not more than once a week.
2. Experiment with your CV title. You will notice that one CV title is clicked more often than another.
3. Also be creative about how you use your CV title! This is your first chance to get noticed.
4. Some job boards allow you to leave an anonymous CV e.g. not showing your full name or last employer. But it is better not to anonymize your CV. It is generally acceptable for you to place your CV on job boards without there being a need to make it anonymous. Besides, recruiters are not keen on anonymous CVs since they usually get no response when they send the owner a message.
5. Mask your age by summarizing the period before 2000 (name only employers and positions).
6. Check the spelling of your text and keep the sentences short and businesslike. Do not use chat language or chat symbols (like smileys). Toiling over your CV for a couple of hours at a stretch can lead to you over-

looking things. Let someone else look at your CV, or print it out and read it carefully the next day for a fresh opinion.

There are thousands of job boards. These vary from generic sites and local regional sites, to niche websites that focus on a certain function group or branch. Niche job boards are becoming increasingly important because these are being used more often by recruiters and jobseekers. They also offer more added value to the target group by collecting relevant news, initiating discussions, promoting events, or focusing attention on professional courses or trainings. This trend will only gain importance in the future.

TIP: There are websites that help you to produce visually striking CVs, like www.VisualCV.com. If you have a creative spirit, or are a marketeer or website designer, do not hesitate to produce something unique. The ultimate form of self-expression is via your own website, preferably linked to a URL with your name (http://www.firstnamesurname.com), which you can also include in your LinkedIn profile. In this way you can exert maximum influence over your personal branding strategy.

3.4 RECRUITMENT AGENCIES AND HEADHUNTERS

The use of recruitment and selection agencies or intermediaries for freelancers and interim managers provides several benefits. These agencies typically employ experienced specialists in a professional area and/or branch, provide services to several customers and clients at the same time, are more active (than the recruiting companies themselves) in database searching, provide objective feedback, are professionals in selection interviews, and also have a commercial interest in acting as intermediaries for you as an individual.

Recruitment and selection agencies typically work on the basis of a success *fee*, in other words, *no cure no pay.* If they are successful in placing someone, they earn 20 – 25% of the candidate's annual salary, which in practice amounts to three months' salary. Recruitment and selection agencies that work in this way often have to compete with other similar agencies. So it is possible that you are approached by different companies for the same position. It is advisable therefore, to always ask who their client is *before* you give them permission to submit your CV in order to avoid problems later on.

Warning: In the contingency recruitment segment you will find agencies that spend as little time as possible on the screening of candidates. They are tempted to propose candidates who might not be ideally suited for the position as well. The added value of these parties is minimal during the selection process; so it is often useless building up a long-term relationship with them. There is not much wrong with this approach though. These agencies are hired by companies as an extra recruitment channel, because the companies themselves lack the expertise or manpower to conduct intensive file searches or internet research. You can recognize this type of agencies by their anonymous advertising of vacancies (the name of the client is usually not specified).
Focus your attention instead on the agencies that have a strong market position (high numbers of vacancies in a niche market), or work on terms of exclusivity. You can search LinkedIn to see whether the consultant of that agency has any *Recommendations*. This is an indication of the reliability of such a person.

As mentioned just previously, there are also recruitment and selection agencies that work on the basis of exclusivity: there is just one agency responsible for the assignment. These agencies often advertise with the name of the client, and usually charge a fixed amount for the effort they put into the search once they have been granted the assignment. The major advantage for clients is that these agencies can offer more quality because the time pressure and competition are less intense. The risk that such a recruitment and selection agency will not succeed in filling the vacancy is very low, since the agency will usually only accept an assignment if they expect to find a suitable candidate. Their selection procedure is also more thorough.

Executive search agencies – or headhunters – work in the same way. These agencies are usually hired to find suitable candidates for management- and top management positions with a basic salary ranging between 80,000 and one million euros or more. Because these agencies follow an extremely intensive trajectory during the entire recruitment and selection procedure, their charges are also higher. A typical commission ranges from 28% to 33% of the annual income. Generally, payments are collected at three points in the recruitment trajectory; one third of the expected fee is requested at the start of the process, one third as soon as the first candidates are interviewed, and the remaining third once a candidate is selected for the position.

In principle, headhunters do *not* advertise.

In stead, they make intensive use of file search and their own network. Important recruitment channels employed by headhunters include:

- references via their personal and business network
- file search in their own candidate database
- research via news articles, magazines and LinkedIn

3.5 WORKING WITH RECRUITERS; INSIDE TIPS

Many job applicants find it frustrating when they do not receive any response to their application. And justifiably so. According to random tests, job applicants receive no response to one in two of their applications. With increasing shortages in the labour market, this situation is unlikely to improve very much. Recruiters and personnel officers have to deal with a big increase in the number of applications, and focus their attention on the potentially successful candidates. A complaint that is often heard concerning recruitment and selection agencies is that they can be irritating – sometimes even aggressive – if they need you, but do not contact you again after an interview. Another complaint is that sometimes they do not even understand what the position entails. Are these practices acceptable?

The first thing every jobseeker needs to know is that the recruitment consultant is working for the client, that the agency has a commercial interest in championing the interests of the client. It is the consultant's responsibility to ensure that the best possible candidate is put forward.
The second thing is that an agency reviews and considers many candidates. Thanks to the internet and online professional networking sites such as LinkedIn, the labour market has become increasingly transparent and competition has grown. A headhunter can afford to be selective. He spends his precious time only on candidates with the required skill set, experience or qualifications. Time is money and he cannot afford to console each and every unsuitable candidate or answer every job application personally (standard responses are usually resorted to in such cases).

If you are talking to a recruiter, it can happen that you occasionally get the feeling that the recruiter does not fully understand the requirements of the job. This is because the vacancy intake was not performed correctly or that some information is lacking. This is not necessarily the fault of the recruiter. While it is the recruiter's task to collect as much information about the position as possible, too often vacancies are simply put out before recruiters have a chance to gain sufficient insight into the work involved when they start searching for suitable candidates. And it has also been known for a manager to modify the requirements during the selection process as a result of insights gained during the process. So it is usually not an advantage to be one of the first candidates to be interviewed. Clients will generally want to see several candidates before making any decisions. Taking all this into account then, keeping in mind the following points can help one make optimal use of recruiters and LinkedIn. :

1. Make sure that the recruiter has received your CV, but do not immediately take any other actions. It is no use starting up a discussion, as this will only annoy the recruiter. The client needs time to study and evaluate your CV.
2. Send your CV in Word format rather than as a PDF or a LinkedIn URL. The client wants to be able to save your CV in digital form so that keyword searches can be used at a later stage.
3. Make sure that you are qualified for the position. If the company is

looking for someone with ten years experience, then they mean ten years and not six or eight. If they want people with a degree in chemistry, they are not interested in a visual arts graduate.

4. In a telephone interview, give short answers to the questions addressed to you. Do not elaborate on unrelated issues, but make sure you convince the recruiter that you are the solution to their problem.

5. In the subsequent phase you will have to demonstrate that you have the skills and abilities required, and show how professional you are. Showing enthusiasm and passion for your profession is extremely important. Prepare thoroughly and do your homework. This will make the crucial difference and set you apart from the many other candidates.

6. Contact the recruiter after your interview with the client (or manager). If you give the impression that you are indifferent about the job or assignment, the client will switch focus to another candidate showing more interest. What is even more important is that you must always respond quickly to any communication from the recruiter or client.

7. If you are offered the position, make sure that you receive as much information as possible about primary and secondary employment conditions. That is the only way you will be able to make a well-reasoned decision. Do not make the mistake of only comparing gross monthly salaries. Secondary employment conditions often make up 40% of the total package.

8. If you are rejected, ask why, so that you can learn from the experience. But do not take it personally and do not become defensive. The final decision does not lie with the recruiter but with the manager or client. The recruiter may well consider you an excellent candidate, and if this is the case, you will be the first to be contacted if another suitable position becomes available!

TIP: *Last but not least*, do not forget that the purpose of a CV is mainly to encourage potential clients to offer you an interview. It is the interview that is decisive!

Useful sources for finding interesting and excellent recruitment and selection agencies include:

1. References via your network and LinkedIn
2. Job boards; approach the agencies that advertise regularly in your field
3. Personnel departments of current or potential employers, ask them which agencies they work with
4. Google and other search engines; study both, the natural search results (left-hand column) and the sponsored links (right-hand column)

TIP: You can also use LinkedIn in many different ways to identify a good recruitment and selection agency, for example, via the *Answer module* (the Q&A forum on LinkedIn) or in a relevant group. Sending your personal network a message asking for advice is also a quick and effective way.

3.6 RECRUITMENT VIA LINKEDİN

In the next three chapters, we will lay the foundation for using LinkedIn to maximum effect through a good profile, a strong and active network, and job application tips. For a number of reasons, we will begin with creating or improving a good profile, not only with the view of lining up an interview and ultimately a job or assignment, but primarily to make it easy for others to find you on the internet in general, and via LinkedIn in particular. LinkedIn is a totally different concept from a job board, and you will need to become active in networking to make the most of it. So don't wait until an appropriate job comes up, but actively look for the right individuals that can help you further your career. And LinkedIn is the ideal tool to help you achieve this.

The second reason you need to have a good profile on LinkedIn is that recruiters are constantly looking for them. The *post and pray* model of job boards – advertise and hope that someone responds – does not apply to

LinkedIn. Of course these options are available with LinkedIn, but it is not its essence. The strength of LinkedIn lies in the collection of profiles, and the inter-relationships that exist. Whereas in the past, specialized recruitment and selection agencies had the advantage of their extensive CV databases, the labour market has become much more transparent now, due to, amongst other things, the sheer numbers of profiles on LinkedIn. Thanks to LinkedIn's *Search People – Advanced* option, a large percentage of the working population has become easily and directly accessible. And recruiters gladly make abundant, free, and unhindered use of this enormous profile database.

How recruiters find the profiles they need on LinkedIn

If recruiters want to find profiles that are useful to them, they work with the *Advanced People Search* function. Using the right search criteria, they are able to find suitable candidates – which could be you.

The search criteria that recruiters may use on LinkedIn to identify if you are a potential candidate for the position they are interested in filling, include:

- keywords that can be found throughout your complete profile
- location
- current job title
- a company you have worked for or currently work for
- the education and training you have followed or are following
- the industry or the branch you work in
- one of the many groups in which the recruiters themselves are active
- language

For you as a jobseeker, freelancer or interim manager, the challenge lies in being found for those jobs for which you wish to be found, at the appropriate moment. And if you are ultimately the best candidate for the job, be aware that references from the people you have worked with can be found on LinkedIn with just one mouse-click. This is done via *Reference Search*, a special option that recruiters on LinkedIn use or can use. Within a couple of mouse-clicks, recruiters can find for example, who worked at a certain company between 2000 and 2002, and they can quickly track your old colleagues and contact them for a reference. Traditionally, when recruiters made a phone call for a reference, they would get responses such as: 'Oh, that was such a long time ago.' But today, this answer is unacceptable; in an instant recruiters can see, all the individuals that are connected to you, which is a very good reason for exercising control over your public profile and recommendations. In other words, keep control over your public testimonial!

Note: To carry out a *Reference Search*, it does not make any difference whether you have your own LinkedIn profile or not – recruiters will always be able to find a couple of your colleagues or ex-colleagues who do!

Linked in ®   Home   Profile   Contacts   Groups   Jobs   Inbox (5)   More...   People ▾   🔍 Advanced

Advanced People Search   [Reference Search]   Saved Searches   Saved Profiles

Need more information about potential employees, employers, and business partners? Enter company names and the years the person worked at each company. Your search will find the people in your network who can provide professional references for your candidate. If the candidate is still with the company, enter 2010. More search tips

Please enter at least one company.

Company name: Years:

Company name		Years		
[ ]		[ ]	to	[ ]
[ ]		[ ]	to	[ ]
[ ]		[ ]	to	[ ]
[ ]		[ ]	to	[ ]
[ ]		[ ]	to	[ ]

[Search]

4. Profile

LinkedIn consists of a number of essential elements:

- Your profile: your public CV and testimonial
- Your updates, newsletter or 'microblog'
- Your existing contacts and the options of finding and inviting new ones
- Your labour market: where would you like to work, who are the recruiters
- Extras

We advise you to build up your LinkedIn presence in stages. For finding new work and assignments, a good profile is the first step. Start by creating your LinkedIn account on www.linkedin.com, filling in your e-mail address and password.

Then you can start filling in your personal data.

Your home page is the central page for all the actions you will be taking:

To start creating your profile, click on the *Profile* option.

4.1 CREATING A PROFILE

Your *Profile* is your public CV; everyone who wants to view it will be able to do so. Your standard CV therefore, forms an excellent basis for your profile on LinkedIn.

The profile is crucial in your labour market approach:

1. It should let everyone see *up-to-date* information on you at first glance, on the first page.
2. It should give a clear idea of the contribution you can make and where you can be *of use*.
3. You should be proud of it and able to answer any questions about it.

Your profile represents who you are and should be focussed on the work you are looking for. This means that your LinkedIn profile is also like a flyer that has to trigger people – without them having seen you – want to contact you for that special position or assignment that you are after. As with your CV, you should write your LinkedIn profile based on your work experience up till now, and geared towards the work you want to do in the future. Whereas on a CV the first page plays the key role, in your LinkedIn profile it is the *Summary* that is crucial. When people search your name via Google, your LinkedIn profile summary will appear high on the web page, and you will have made your first impression already!

It takes time to create a professional profile – 'a whole Sunday' is fairly common – but you will find that it is definitely worth the investment. According to LinkedIn statistics, users with profiles that have been completed 100% are viewed up to 40 times more often than profiles that are only partially complete. And always make sure you keep your profile up to date, because an outdated profile is like an outdated CV, with one essential difference – everybody can see it!

Employers will only approach you if they see a complete and up-to-date picture of you; an outdated profile will even be deliberately ignored. So every time there is a change in your professional circumstances, remember to adapt your public profile on LinkedIn accordingly.

TIP: Professional assistance in creating your profile on LinkedIn can be worth the extra investment. Career coach Aaltje Vincent has found that a self-written CV/profile is generally only 30% effective.

English or ...?

LinkedIn fully supports 6 languages at this moment: English, Spanish, German, Portugese, Italian and French. You will probably be tempted to create your profile in your local language which may be different from these six. There are a few disadvantages to this:

1. LinkedIn is an international business network. If you have international business contacts (say in purchasing or sales for instance), they will not be able to read your profile.
2. Recruiters typically perform searches using English-language terms.
3. There will also usually be a large English-language community in your country that can be useful in promoting your career further.
4. You may be working for a local company at the moment and so a profile in the local language may be quite natural. But be aware that you will need to update your profile in English as soon as you start working for an international company.
5. An English-language profile is a sign to recruiters that you want to work in an international environment.

In other words, in pure professional terms you will probably benefit more from an English-language profile. Of course this choice remains a personal matter. You may still choose to write your LinkedIn profile in your local language if:

- your English is poor
- you have no desire to use the English language for work, not even in a local working environment
- you have no intention to work for an international company or for an international client.

TIP: To save time and maintain clarity and brevity, simply copy and paste the text from your CV onto your LinkedIn profile. Another similar option that LinkedIn offers is: *Import your résumé.* For more details, see chapter 7.

Your photo

A good photo is absolutely essential. According to LinkedIn statistics, profiles that include a photo are viewed 30% more often than those without. A business passport photo engenders more trust, and if you are active on different sites or social media on the internet (own website, Twitter, Facebook), we recommend using the same photo everywhere. LinkedIn is not a network for friends, so a holiday photo is not appropriate.

Personalia

On a standard CV, you will regularly come across subjects like civil status, date of birth, military service, number of children if any, and place of birth. The power of LinkedIn lies in the fact that your expertise is the focus, and that the personalia – justifiably – are of less importance; so you will place these right at the bottom, if at all!

Job title

For your current and previous positions, always choose the most *typical* job title, even if the term used in your contract of employment is different. A job title must be elaborated on, for example because the tasks and responsibilities of an account manager can vary widely from company to company; so use the job title that is most relevant to your own situation. Recruiters mostly perform searches using English-language job titles. If you do not use any English terms, you will miss out on opportunities. We recommend using the typical English term, or a combined job title, such as for example the combined Dutch-English job title: directiesecretaresse/Office manager.

You can use the *Headline* option to mention something extra. For example:

Jacco Valkenburg ①ⁿ 🖪

Employers/Recruiters: Need branding, training, or sourcing help? Contact me and let's discuss how I can support you.

N.B. Sometimes telephone numbers or e-mail addresses are specified next to the name, but this is officially not allowed in LinkedIn and your profile might be suspended.

Summary

> **Summary** [Edit]
>
> None ✚ **Add Summary**
>
> **Specialties:**
> None ✚ **Add Specialties**

As mentioned earlier, the *Summary* is crucial for your LinkedIn profile; it puts you in the picture for the type of work or assignments you are interested in. You can specify a number of things here, but make sure you keep it brief:

1. Your *two minutes of fame,* or *elevator pitch*; outline in short sentences what solution you can offer to which problem.
2. The type of work you are doing now, and the type of work you wish to be approached for. What makes your eyes light up with passion when people talk to you?
3. The 'common thread' of your work experience, which makes the move that you want to make now seem obvious.
4. An explanation for your career switch if any, for example: 'As a result of having had professional career counselling, I have made a conscious choice of becoming an undertaker.'
5. Indicate whether you are open to new work, and the kind of work for which you wish to be approached (or not).

Specialties
This section in your LinkedIn profile is the ideal place to highlight a number of specialities in your work experience, such as:

- Specific knowledge, for example of computer programmes or purchasing in China

- Special work experience, for example on a project for ICT out-sourcing or the merger of two companies
- Your language skills, for example, 'fluent business French with 12 years experience'
- The network you bring with you, for example in the retail sector
- Your experience in speaking at conferences (specify which conferences)
- Your publications, for example in trade journals
- Your public appearances in the newspaper, radio or TV
- Outstanding and relevant sporting achievements or interests

If necessary, use a list with keywords that increase your chances of being found via LinkedIn's search engine (*Advanced Search*).

'Keyword management' means mentioning as many keywords that are applicable to you, as possible. This increases the chance that recruiters find your talent. Think for example of the keywords: team leader, head of department, manager, etc.

Current and Past Experience
Your work experience always consists of two parts, both of which are important:

1. Context: Describe in two sentences who your current employer is, how big the company is, how many people work there, what it does, and where you work (head office, a branch, company division). Use the name that the company has now and not a previous one. Remember that even if you work for one of the best-known companies in your country, it does not necessarily mean that everybody knows the company or has a clear picture of what it does. Make sure that it is clear to everybody, inside and outside your area of expertise, within which context you are working or have worked there.
2. Working day: Put yourself in the profile reader's shoes here. In a few words, perhaps using striking imagery, describe your experience. What were your achievements? Which projects did you work on? Specify how many people you managed, indicate the amounts of any budget or

turnover you were responsible for. In other words, specify exactly and in short sentences what the reader considers the most important, in as few words as possible. What employers want to know is *what you did between nine and five*. Use action-oriented words like *managed, cut back, reduced, achieved, organized*. Stress what you achieved exactly, for example: 'reduced absenteeism from 9% to 5%' rather than 'reduced absenteeism'. Avoid unusual or vague (internal) abbreviations and technical jargon, even though you may be applying for work within your own area of expertise. Replace the (internal) abbreviations with complete words so that you have more relevant search words in your profile.

If you followed a part-time course while you were working, mention this as part of your work experience; this will make your profile much stronger. This course will appear for a second time in the education part of your profile.

If you have any gaps in your work experience, a so-called 'gap in your CV', mention this briefly with a positive description and be prepared to answer questions on it. Examples include:

- Re-assessment of life and work.
- Eight-month trip through North-, Central- and South America.
- Time-out to bring up children.
- Time-out for social activities in sport, environment, education, etc.
- Time-out for a stay in Eastern Europe.
- For a period in which you are unemployed, state that you are, 'in-between jobs', or 'ready for a new challenge', or 'ready for the next step in my career where I can follow my heart' or 'on the way to a new challenge with the aid of professional career counselling'.
- Professional development:
- – studies: coaching, creative career development, counselling
- – work experience: coach, trainer, counsellor (even if these were internships)
- Following a trajectory at a career advice centre as a re-assess-

ment on work and career. The result is a conscious choice to
work for example as a doctor's assistant

Education

Describe the contents of the course(s) you followed, and mention particularly the aspects that fascinated you, or, if relevant, the topic of your doc-
toral thesis. If you have recently taken a course in your area of expertise,
or in another area because you want to make a career switch, then mention this in two places: first when describing the position you were com-
bining with the course you took, and again when listing your education.
As we mentioned earlier, this will make your profile much stronger and
therefore more effective, and rightfully so since you took the course
alongside your work!

Websites

The *Websites* element gives you the opportunity to mention your own, or,
for example, your employer's website. You will be making it easier for
someone to get to know you better by directing them straight to the website link that you consider the most important in providing a good description of you and your work. You can also specify websites corresponding to any leisure time pursuit or voluntary work you are involved in, or
the site of a blog, or a link to a YouTube film. As you can see, there are no re-
strictions in terms of content, so you can be as creative as you want. But
be sure to always keep your personal branding strategy in mind.

Twitter

The *Twitter* section gives you the opportunity to include your Twitter ac-
count(s) and its tweets in your profile.

Contact Settings

You can add your personal data in the *Personal Information* and *Contact
Settings* sections. Recruiters give special attention to your contact information. This is located right at the bottom of your profile. Make absolutely sure that you include your telephone number and e-mail address. This
way you make it much easier for everyone to approach you for a potential
job, for networking purposes or to request extra information. Your birth-

day and your marital status are not relevant to your search for new work; so it is up to you whether you include these or not.

Personal Information [Edit]

Phone:	**Add a phone number** to your profile.
Address:	**Add your address** to your profile.
IM:	**Add an IM** to your profile.
Birthday:	**Add your birthday** to your profile.
Marital status:	**Add your marital status** to your profile.

Contact Settings [Edit]

Give people advice on how you want to be contacted.

Interested In:

career opportunities	consulting offers
new ventures	job inquiries
expertise requests	business deals
reference requests	getting back in touch

TIP: Always list your telephone number and your e-mail address in your profile. This makes it very easy for recruiters to contact you. Make sure your e-mail address looks professional.

Difference between Job Inquiries and Career Opportunities

Many people do not understand the difference between *Job Inquiries* and *Career Opportunities;* so we will explain these in more detail here. With the *Career Opportunities* element you are telling other users that you are open to messages about vacancies or freelance assignments, in other words, you are part of the category of *Potential Employees*, as a search term defined by LinkedIn.

TIP: It is crucial for jobseekers to tick the *Career Opportunities* box. Recruiters can fine-tune their searches, via *Advanced Search*, to the *Potential Employees* category, which generates results of profiles open to *Career Opportunities*.

With the *Job Inquiries* element, a manager or recruiter lets other LinkedIn users know that he/she is open to messages from jobseekers. This is a setting that recruiters and managers should, in principle, always have activated. *Hiring Managers* is the term used by LinkedIn, for profiles in which the *Job Inquiries* option is specified.

TIP: Make use of Hiring Managers to approach a prospective employer, for questions regarding work and vacancies.

N.B. IM stands for *Instant Messaging*. The programmes offering this service ensure that you immediately see and are able to respond to such a message (pop-up). Thus, with an IM programme you can instantly start chatting with someone online. One of the most well-known IM programmes is Skype.

Public profile

Public Profile
Your public profile displays **full** profile information.
http://www.linkedin.com/in/aaltjevincent

In *Settings* (1. upper right header on Linkedin.com) you can define your *Public Profile* (2. to the left).
Your public profile performs a number of crucial functions:

1. You can include your LinkedIn public profile on your standard CV and/or in your letter of application (see page 91).
2. You can even use it in your e-mail signature (see page 91).
3. Or you can use it on your business card.

TIP: If you have a fairly common name, you can also add a job title to it or even replace it. As a freelance specialist or interim manager, this is an outstanding strategy to spread your name and strengthen it. An increasing number of e-recruiters are also using search engines such as Google to look for CVs or profiles that have been placed online. Because Google gives a high priority to LinkedIn profiles, your profile will appear high in any list of search results, and adding your job interests along with your name in the profile title, will also ensure that the search results generates your name in connection with your interests. For example: http://www.linkedin.com/in/johndoecareercoach.

4.2 UPDATE

LinkedIn gives you the option of informing your contacts about your professional status and interests via a *Status Update* (*Share*). You can use this to create:

- Your newsletter: Create a new message every day, week or month about what you are doing at work, what you are thinking about, about articles you have read or interesting sites or blogs you have come across
- Your 'microblog': Exchange professional and up-to-date information, 24 hours a day

The *Update or Share* option is located above your profile; you can update your profile any time you want via the home page. You can also modify your profile using the option *Edit my Profile*, but it is quicker to do so via the home page. Using *Update*, you can let everybody know what you are doing at work and, if you are looking for new work, that you are ready to take a new step. This way it becomes your personal and unique newsletter! Other people also call it a 'microblog'. Your own contacts are automatically notified about your new update, if they visit their home page every day. You can explain the benefits of this 'newsletter function' in LinkedIn in an InMail (see page 92).

TIP: We recommend 'filling' your *Status Update* before inviting your contacts to join your network. Anyone you invite will want to take a look at your profile, and then he/she will be up-to-date with your latest news!

TIP: The symbol that LinkedIn initially used to represent the update is the medieval village square clarion, and later the megaphone. We think this is an ideal image. In our eyes, it encourages the idea of seeing the LinkedIn-update option as your own personal megaphone in your virtual village square! Be well aware though, that your messages have to be relevant in the context of indicating the kind of work you are looking for. For example, do not place any private messages and do not continually 'flood' your village square with news, otherwise you lose people's attention and might irritate your network members.

Also be aware that your updates are a means of leaving a trail on the internet; all your updates will be stored. To come across as a professional and to attract new work, it is wise to remember this every time you are about to enter an update.

Make good use of it. In our experience, updates provoke responses, you are back in the picture for a while, and your contacts may also remember what you have written. It could even mean that you are the one they think of when they hear of an appropriate job vacancy. This really is a fantastic way of maintaining your network, something that is crucial in your job hunt, now, and probably also for the rest of your working life!

Recruiters also follow the updates of all their connections in their areas of specialisation. For them, their connections, such as yourself, are the equivalent of the old-fashioned card index box. Recruiters like following potential candidates by reading their updates. You never know when someone is going to write, 'Versatile organizer required in a start-up? Mail Nancy now!'

Aaltje Vincent on BNR Nieuwsradio from 25th of May on for three weeks every day with #linkedin tips at 10.25am, the14 essential tips for people at work!

Elise Dokkum Available for a job as project assistant in an environment where people are important and a little bit crazy, work is diverse and humour is always around!

Jacco Valkenburg finished writing book about using LinkedIn for job seekers, together with Aaltje Vincent www.SolliciterenviaLinkedIn.nl
2 days ago

Els Ackerman is thinking about organizing a party for her new book 'Help, ik zoek mijn passie' ('Help, where is my passion'), about myths in the world of careercounseling. Look in the bookshop towards the end of june.

As you can see from the examples, the creative possibilities of updates are literally endless. It is a great way to communicate with your personal network, and there is evidence that people respond to them, either straight away with a response via LinkedIn, or later on 'in real life', when they next meet you and ask 'How's the project going? I saw from your last update that you're working on that merger.'

4.3 RECOMMENDATIONS: REQUESTING AND GIVING THEM

"It was great to work with Arjen Mollee during the World Outgames in Montréal. He quickly made his priority known and we figured out how we could best help each other to ensure the successful coverage of this event in Europe. A great personality, an attention to details, very professional and easy to get along with, would best describe him." *June 1, 2010*

(2ⁿᵈ) Eric Prud'Homme, *Bénévole, Outgames*
      worked directly with Arjen at 1st worldOutgames Montréal 2006

You have now taken your first steps in career management via LinkedIn:

- Your profile: your public CV
- Your update, newsletter or 'microblog'

You have created your profile geared towards the new step that you want to take in your working life, and you have now made your CV public. Anyone who wants to read it, can do so. Fantastic, that is the essence of LinkedIn!

Important: Now we come to 'your public testimonial'. During the job application procedure, employers often ask for references, and they normally contact these references by phone. Usually, you would have warned your ex-colleague or manager beforehand which job applications you are involved in, and would have told them whom they might expect a telephone call from. You also discuss which qualities and aspects of your work experience you want them to highlight.

Well, nowadays the person giving you a reference can do that in *public* by placing a *Recommendation* on LinkedIn. The *Recommendations* option is devised to serve exactly such a purpose. It is an important element because recruiters read these recommendations! When recruiters are looking for candidates via *Advanced Search,* profiles with recommendations are ranked higher in the search results; these profiles will even have an extra little 'flag'. In other words, these profiles will already have a head start over the rest. Ask yourself what you would do: you see fifty profiles and five of them have a little flag next to them indicating that they have been recommended. Which ones would you read first?

Additionally, recruiters can also find people who have worked with you and who could therefore provide you with a reference, very easily via LinkedIn. That is why we recommend that you explicitly approach people in your network to write a recommendation for you. That way you keep control of the situation and you increase the value of your profile enormously.

TIP: Ask for recommendations! Otherwise you will not get any, just as is the case with normal references. Shatter that mask of modesty; if you want to get into the frame for some new work, you will have to put yourself in the spotlight, with all your qualities and positive references. Ask someone to be an 'ambassador' for you, and become one yourself.

Asking for a recommendation

You ask for a recommendation as you would with a 'normal' reference, in person, when you meet someone or speak to them on the phone. It will be enormously appreciated, and you can discuss straight away which qualities you would like them to recommend in particular. So avoid the use of the standard invitations that LinkedIn offers. You can also arrange for the recommendation text to be sent to you by e-mail first. This gives you the opportunity to discuss it, and once you are both satisfied with the final version, the other person can place it on LinkedIn.

At that same moment you will receive the recommendation via LinkedIn, and once you have accepted it, it will automatically be placed on your profile. Correspondingly, a message will appear in the profile of the person recommending you, indicating that this person has given you a reference. If you are not satisfied with a recommendation, you can refuse it by archiving it, or have it modified via the option *Request Replacement*, for example, if your career has taken a different path and you want to highlight other qualities of yourself.

Giving a recommendation

You can also give recommendations to people with whom you collaborated with good results, or with whom you worked on a project; to an outstanding secretary; to a fine colleague with whom you achieved a successful reorganization, or whom you gave a training course. This way, you put both yourself and the other person in the spotlight. Giving recommendations to prominent professional peers with whom you have worked, like professors, innovative entrepreneurs and authoritative managers, says something about your education and work experience. You give a recommendation by going to the profile of a first-line connection, then clicking on the link 'Recommend this person' located in the top right-hand corner.

"Jacco knows that in the recruitment business you always have to look for new ways to get in touch with talented people. By writing the book 'Recruitment via LinkedIn' for Dutch HR-professionals Jacco has shown that he understands his business and he is not afraid to share his knowlegde so that other reciuters can benefit and improve their own work."
May 20, 2008

(2nd) Stefan Tibben, *Hoofdredacteur P&Oactueel, Reed Business (voorheen Reed Business Information)*
was with another company when working with Jacco on Recruitment via LinkedIn

Mutual recommendation

We are regularly asked the question: 'Do you always have to return the compliment of being recommended by someone, by recommending that person in return?' LinkedIn offers this option by default. You receive a recommendation, and after you have accepted the recommendation, LinkedIn offers you the option to recommend the other person in return. Our advice is to be cautious with this; LinkedIn is a representation of 'real life', and in 'real life', finding 'jobs for the boys' is always frowned upon. If you decide to return the favour, then allow a reasonable amount of time to pass between receiving a recommendation and giving one to the same person. This is because all the new recommendations are placed on your home page, and if you give each other a recommendation on the same day, all your contacts will be able to see it, making it appear rather like fixed-up statements than genuine recommendations.

Content of your recommendation

Ask for recommendations that add value to your LinkedIn profile, so that it attracts the attention of people in a position to offer you new work. Make your recommendation concrete. For example: 'As a result of the collaboration with Paul, the project was completed three months earlier than scheduled', or: 'John achieved a 15% decrease in the purchasing of office supplies', or: 'Anna is a good coach, I happily refer employees to her. She always know how to hit exactly the right tone, so that they come back to me with a concrete personal development plan.'

4.4 GROUPS

Many professionals participate in business networks, company social events, conferences and other events, student, alumni and university associations as part of their daily lives, in order to gain and maintain business contacts. That is now possible via LinkedIn; people find each other and engage in discussions through the many groups on LinkedIn. Here too, LinkedIn resembles 'real life'; you meet each other and you share information with each other.

We strongly recommend taking part in groups for a number of reasons, given below. All the following six points will be explained in more detail in the next chapters.

1. Groups are mentioned, together with their logo, on your profile (optional). It is a way of raising your profile and giving the impression of being an active professional.
2. You will be able to see the complete profiles of all the group members, even if they are not yet personally connected to you. You can also easily and quickly invite them to connect with you.
3. You can send members a free InMail directly. An InMail is an e-mail you send via LinkedIn (see page 92). You will not be bothered much by spam because the group members are not allowed to send a message to all the members at once.
4. You are kept updated on all the activities within the group, as well as, for example, the discussions currently going on.

5. The group manager can send an announcement to everyone, just as with any other membership, about, for example, an upcoming conference.

6. Recruiters and 'hiring managers' (those managers who need a new staff member) make full use of the LinkedIn groups. They benefit from them in a number of ways:

a. They look up the group members and may find good candidates for their vacancies
b. They view profiles of the people who take part in *discussions*; these people stand out as being committed and possessing expertise
c. They place their vacancies on group discussions (*Jobs*, see page 85).

Although there is an enormous number of groups on LinkedIn that you can join, you are not allowed join more than fifty. Make the maximum use of this facility as it is one of the most intensively used options on LinkedIn!

 Recruitment Consultants and Staffing Professionals   Already a member
This is a group only for Corporate Staffing Professionals, (Agency) Recruiters, HR
Managers, HRM Directors and Employer Branding Experts to expand our network of people, ideas
and share leads. Please feel free to join this dedicated Recruiter group on LinkedIn. For Recruiters,
by Recruiters.
Yesterday's Activity: Discussions (2) News (5) Jobs (5)
Owner: **Jacco Valkenburg** | 46,139 members | Share

You can find the groups that are most relevant for you in the following ways:

1. Look at profiles of people you know in your area of expertise. The groups they take part in can be a good source for your own personal selection.
2. Use the *Search Groups* option and do a search on keywords.

TIP: Think hard about which groups are relevant for your professional development and profile. Take part in the discussions, place articles, and take a look at *Jobs* (see page 88) regularly.

Via the main menu *Groups – My Groups*, you will find all the groups that you are a member of. You can go to the website of the relevant group from here, view the members, or withdraw your membership from the group via *Settings*.

TIP: In Groups, under the tab *Jobs*, you will find all the jobs that have been posted. The number of jobs varies enormously, but it remains an excellent direct source of finding vacancies!

4.5 IMPORTANT TIPS

Here is a summary of the most important tips for creating and raising your profile:

1. Create a profile in the language that is most appropriate for your ambitions. Recruiters prefer an English-language profile. If you use a language other than English for your profile, make sure you add English-language keywords in your summary.
2. Add a professional photo; your profile will be viewed 30% more frequently if you do.
3. Pay a lot of attention to your summary; keep it short and to the point. This is the first impression that others will get of you!
4. Describe your area of specialization: what makes you unique compared to the rest of the candidates?

5. Make your public profile link stand out (for example www.linkedin. com/in/johndoe).
6. Give a results-focussed description of your current and previous positions and employers.
7. Recommend others (*Recommendations*).
8. Ask for recommendations from the employers mentioned in your profile. Do not be too modest, try to get at least three recommendations, you will end up higher in the search results, initiated by recruiters on LinkedIn.
9. Add information such as interests if this will make your profile stronger in terms of work.
10. Indicate explicitly when and how people can get in touch with you (under *Contact Settings*); recruiters will want to call or e-mail you directly.
11. Add your blog or presentation via *LinkedIn Applications* (see page 104).
12. And... don't forget that LinkedIn is a public platform. Make sure there are no spelling mistakes and avoid typos!

5. Networking with LinkedIn

5.1 LinkedIn as a network tool

You have now taken the following steps in career management via LinkedIn:

- Your profile: your public CV and testimonial
- Your update, newsletter or 'microblog'

You now have a complete profile that is geared towards the kind of work you are looking for. At the same time, your *Status Update* is up-to-date with a news item that everybody can read. You are now ready to build your network of contacts. If you are looking for new work, your contacts – and their contacts – are absolutely essential, as we made clear in section 1.4.

The most important motivational factors for users of LinkedIn are establishing contacts and communicating with each other. LinkedIn is based on relations and trust, and the motto, 'the more you put into it, the more you will get out of it', definitely holds for LinkedIn. It is a fantastic *tool* for your network activities, and on top of that, it is free, online and available 24 hours a day.

LinkedIn is effective for networking because you already have access to a lot of information before you even make your first contact, as is evident from your own profile. Who are you, who do you know, what are you doing at the moment, and how can people get in touch with you? For millions of people, this will now be perfectly clear and transparent. This way, you can network more professionally and maintain your relations more efficiently than, for example, at that one-off social event or some annual conference, where in the best case scenario, you will speak to a couple of people who might perhaps some day be useful to you. LinkedIn enables you to gain more information upfront and makes it easier to meet new people through a mutual contact.

According to the English anthropologist Robin Dunbar, the maximum number of stable social relationships anyone is able to maintain is 148. This is the assumed cognitive limit (Dunbar's number) to the number of contacts that a person can maintain social relationships with, on condition that all the relations make an effort to do so. If you become an active participant in online social networking, it becomes impractical to talk regularly on the phone to all your contacts for half an hour. But you can send instant messages, mails or updates at lightning fast speeds, and still manage to keep in touch with everyone. That is one of the great things about online networking; you can breathe new life into your old contacts, and the 'acquisition' of new contacts, and maintaining a relationship becomes much easier. This way you can beat Dunbar's number and expand the social group size without a commensurate cost in time spent.

5.2 REFERRAL RECRUITMENT

Companies favour recruitment through referrals, networking, or informal contacts. This type of recruitment implies cases where potential candidates are suggested and hired following recommendations from the company's own employees and their friends, family or acquaintances, but also through recommendations from suppliers and clients. Referral recruitment involves the use of informal networks to attract new employees through word-of-mouth contacts. The person to propose an applicant, who finally ends up being hired, will be rewarded (typically a fixed amount made known beforehand).

The advantages of referral recruitment to the organization are obvious:

- Thanks to *inside information* the applicants will be well-informed and committed
- It is personal, direct and quick
- The recruitment costs are low
- The own employees are closely involved in recruiting good quality colleagues

It goes without saying that LinkedIn makes referral recruitment even easier and quicker. The supplier can now say: 'I know a good new employee for your sales department; just take a look at John Doe's LinkedIn profile. I read recently that he was on the lookout for a new step in his career.'

5.3 YOUR CONNECTIONS

'How many connections can/should you have, or are you allowed to have on LinkedIn?' is a Frequently Asked Question. There are many different opinions about what kind of connections (quality) and how many connections (quantity) are ideal. Let's look at this issue more closely.

Quality

We are assuming that you consider qualitative connections important while using LinkedIn, and that you are using, or want to use, LinkedIn in order to place yourself in the spotlight for new work. Networking with the purpose of being placed in the spotlight for new work should begin with drawing an accurate picture of all the people you already know. Take a professional attitude towards this and consider your classmates (current and/or previous), your colleagues (current and/or previous), fellow-members of your professional association, participants at a congress you attended, and your private contacts who can also prove important for you in your work. You should realize that these people can be interesting contacts because they know you well *and* are therefore in a good position to be your ambassador. All your contacts also know other – different – contacts, and can help you further if they hear of a vacancy by introducing you in the relevant circles of which they are already members.

LinkedIn categorizes contacts according to degrees, indicated by the symbol:

1. The people you invite and who accept your invitation are your first-degree contacts, or connections

2. The people that these connections have as first-degree contacts (but who are not your first-degree contacts) are your second-degree contacts
3. The people your second-degree contacts have as first-degree contacts are your third-degree contacts

There are two great advantages to quality contacts on LinkedIn. Having a good circle of first-degree contacts on LinkedIn ensures that firstly, via your own home page, you can follow these first-degree contacts and keep them informed via *Update*, for example, by letting them know that you are ready for a new challenge in your career.

The second benefit is that via your first-degree contacts, you can see how you can get in touch with your second-degree contacts.

For example, say the co-author of this book, Aaltje Vincent, who lives in Almere, would really like to be personally introduced to the mayor of the city, Annemarie Jorritsma. When she types Jorritsma's name in *Search People*, she finds Annemarie Jorritsma's profile and sees that she can ask Joep Kramer or Yvonne van Mierlo (her first-degree contacts) for an introduction. She can send a message via LinkedIn but she can also call them personally of course.

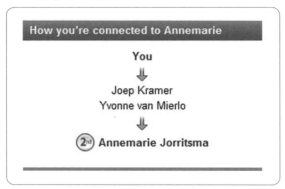

LinkedIn does not show any of your contacts beyond the third degree (in other words, where there are three or more links in between you and the other person). There are two ways of viewing the profiles of these people who are 'further away':

a. If they belong to the same LinkedIn Group as yourself, you can see their *Full Profile*
b. If you know their name, you can view their *Public Profile* via Google

TIP: Think very carefully about all the people you know and who they know, from colleagues and ex-classmates, to your friends. Ask yourself the question: 'Which of these people could be an ambassador for me in my search for new work?'

Quantity

Apart from quality, quantity, or rather diversity plays an important role in an effective network. Firstly, it is good to have contacts totally outside your 'familiar circle'. The more first-degree contacts know that you are looking for new work, the more second-degree contacts they will be able to inform about your unmistakable talents! Secondly, the more contacts you have, the more opportunities you will have to view other people's profiles and see how you can get in touch with them. Ask yourself the question: 'Is LinkedIn really important when it comes to people I already know so well and vice versa? Or are the connections you make with people you do not know so well, more valuable on LinkedIn, for that very reason?'

On LinkedIn you will come across profiles where the abbreviation LION is prominently displayed. LION – *LinkedIn Open Networker* – is nothing more than a sign for other users that this person will accept invitations from anyone who wants to connect with him/her. LIONs can also often be recognized by the fact that they are members of one of the many LION groups, and that they have over 500 connections. The top LIONs are real super connectors, with even more than 10,000 contacts. The maximum number of connections that LinkedIn allows is 30,000.

Through your first-degree contacts, you can view the complete profiles of their second-degree and third-degree contacts, and you can see which first-degree connections will be able to introduce you to a second- or third-degree connection. It goes without saying that you will be able to see a lot more peoples' complete profiles through a few LIONs and super connectors. And who knows, you might just have a job interview with someone who might otherwise have been outside your network, but now falls inside it. So the best approach is to identify the LIONs and super connectors in your area of expertise, for example via a group, and to invite them to connect with you.

With his contacts, Jacco Valkenburg, co-author and recruiter, can view almost 30% of all profiles on LinkedIn, or approach the owners of those profiles for a vacancy. For him as a recruiter, a 'wide reach' on LinkedIn is invaluable. You can view your own network statistics via the main menu *Contacts – Network Statistics*:

Imported Contacts	Profile Organizer	**Network Statistics**	Add Connections

Here you see statistics about your network, including how many users you can reach through your connections. Your network grows every time you add a connection — invite connections now.

Your Network of Trusted Professionals

You are at the center of your network. Your connections can introduce you to 13,841,400+ professionals — here's how your network breaks down:

1	**Your Connections** Your trusted friends and colleagues	997
2	**Two degrees away** Friends of friends; each connected to one of your connections	462,200+
3	**Three degrees away** Reach these users through a friend and one of their friends	13,378,100+
	Total users you can contact through an Introduction	13,841,400+

40,135 new people in your network since January 21

TIP: Having many connections can potentially put you into the frame of many LinkedIn participants and you will have access to many profiles. Make a conscious decision about the ideal ratio of quality versus quantity that you want to work towards.

5.4 WHO HAS VIEWED MY PROFILE?

Once you have created your profile the way you like it, and you have informed your contacts in a professional way, you will notice that your profile will be viewed more frequently. Before you improve your profile further and invite more contacts, you can set a benchmark. *How often is your profile being viewed at the moment?* And you can then continue to track this.

What benefit does the *Who has viewed my profile* function have if you are looking for new work? You can click on it to see who has viewed your profile. Two possibilities here:

1. The name of the person and the company name who viewed your profile is shown.
2. The profile viewer has opted to remain anonymous

Recruiters typically use the option of showing their full name when viewing a profile. So this is a special, unique opportunity to make contact with this recruiter and establish the possible mutual benefits of your contact.

TIP: We recommend that you follow up with a telephone call to any recruiter who has viewed your profile, and use the opportunity of the direct, personal contact to discuss relevant issues.

How do you want to appear to others?

You too will view many profiles of other LinkedIn users. How visible do you want to be to them? Anonymous, or with your name and company name, or not visible at all?

The default setting in LinkedIn is that everyone can view any profile on LinkedIn anonymously. When it comes to choosing the extent of visibility you prefer however, there are three options, and you are free to choose the one you want. This can be done in the following manner:

1. In the upper right-hand corner of your screen, click on Settings.
    Under Privacy Settings in the right-hand column, click on Profile Views.

2.

> **What will be shown to other LinkedIn users when you view their profiles?**
>
> ◉ Show my name and headline
> ○ Only show my anonymous profile characteristics, such as industry and title
> ○ Don't show users that I've viewed their profile

This is where you can make your choice; we have both selected *Show my Name and headline*, and our experience is that it ensures that our profiles get viewed more frequently. In other words, it generates 'traffic' on our profiles and therefore leads to more dialogues and real contacts.

5.5 FINDING CONNECTIONS

There are at least seven ways of finding 'old acquaintances' via LinkedIn and connecting with them. These are:

1. Using Outlook, Apple Mail or other e-mail programmes
2. Using hotmail.com, gmail.com or other web-based mail programmes
3. Searching for Colleagues
4. Searching for Classmates
5. Through the Invite contacts option
6. Through the Browser Toolbar
7. By means of an Individual search

We will discuss all the possibilities here in further detail. Start from the main menu *Contacts* option, or go to www.linkedIn.com/findcontacts.

1. *Contacts – Imported Contacts – Import your desktop email contacts* (importing contacts via Outlook): This is a fantastic method because you can immediately see:
   a. Which of your (Outlook address book) contacts are not on LinkedIn
   b. Which of them *are* on LinkedIn; they are marked with an IN icon.

You can now directly link your profile to the people who are already registered – see IN icon – by ticking the checkbox next to their name. You can also easily invite the contacts that LinkedIn does not recognize, to join your network by sending them a message.

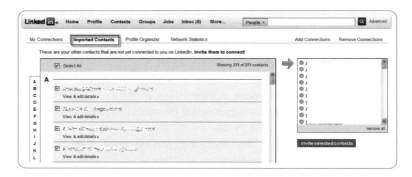

2. *Contacts – Imported Contacts – Searching your email contacts*: *hot-mail.com, gmail.com, yahoo.com* (importing contacts via webmail): You can also import connections from Gmail, Hotmail and Yahoo. But make sure that you keep your password secret, otherwise someone else could export all your contacts!

3. *Contacts – Add Connections – Colleagues*: You can add colleagues from your current and previous jobs. With one click you can find all the employees at your previous or current company who have registered with LinkedIn.

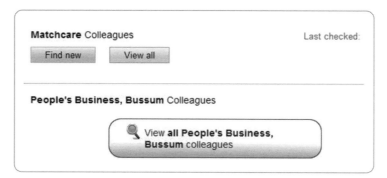

4. *Contacts – Add Connections – Classmates*: Classmates from courses you are taking or have taken, from current or previous schools, can also be added to your contacts on LinkedIn. When you choose a school, a list of names of people who graduated in a certain year or who studied in the exact same period as yourself, will appear.

TIP: Add all your active e-mail addresses to your LinkedIn profile, so that old friends, classmates and ex-colleagues can find you on LinkedIn. You can add them in the following manner: Click on *Settings* and in the right-hand column under *Personal Information* you will see *Email Addresses*.

5. *Contacts – Add Connections – Enter Email Addresses*: As described in the previous tip, you can also invite contacts on LinkedIn via their e-mail addresses. If you enter the name and e-mail address of your contacts, you can invite a number of people at the same time.

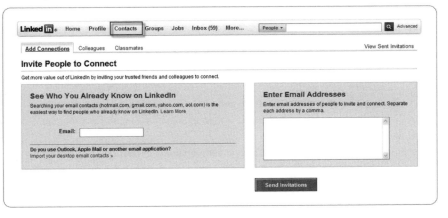

6. *Tools – Browser Toolbar* (look right at the bottom of your home page) : This option is available for Internet Explorer and Firefox. Go to any web-site of your choice, select a company name, and by clicking the right mouse button, you will see all the contact persons that work there. You get immediate and instant access to LinkedIn, and will be able to search rapidly within your network.

7. *Individual:* You can search for people you want to specifically find, and invite them as well:
   a. Via *Search People:* Type the name of the person you are looking for and send him/her an invitation.
   b. Via your contacts: Who are the first-degree contacts of the person you are looking for, and which of these first-degree contacts can introduce you to him/her?
   c. Via your groups: You can carry out a search on individuals within the groups of which you are a member. Which of the members would you like to have as first-degree network connections?
   d. Via *Advanced People Search:* Using this option you can search for peers in your field, for example: Keyword: *scientist,* and Industry: *alternative medicine*
   e. Via the option *Viewers of this profile also viewed:* This option can be found on the right, next to your profile. People who viewed your profile also viewed profiles of others which were similar to yours, or profiles that you have viewed as well. These people could be a source of new contacts.
   f. Via *People you may know:* This option is found on the upper right-hand corner of your home page. This can also be a source of new contacts. LinkedIn gives an estimate of the number of people on LinkedIn based on 'common characteristics', and mentions names that may be relevant here. It is always worthwhile taking a regular look at this option.
   g. Via the option *Who has viewed my profile?:* This option is located to the right on the home page. These are people who have viewed your profile; they may include a recruiter. It is always worth making contact and establishing any possible mutual benefits with the people who are displayed under this option.

5.6 INVITING CONNECTIONS

You have now taken the following steps in career management via LinkedIn:

- Your profile: your public CV and testimonial.
- Your update, newsletter or 'microblog'.
- Finding your contacts.

We have now come to an important step in the LinkedIn process: sending invitations to contacts. We once again recommend that you only do this *after* you have completed your profile, and after you have created a good *Update*. The chance that someone you invite will view your profile is extremely high. Take advantage of this moment, build a good profile of yourself in your *Summary* and your *Update* and make sure that both of these are geared towards finding new work, so that other people automatically thin: 'That job I heard about last week, that's ideal for John!', and: 'Oh, that's convenient, we can make good use of John here!'

Invitation texts

In our experience, your contacts will appreciate a more personal touch to the standard LinkedIn invitation text, and they will then, more likely, accept your invitation.

Group invitation

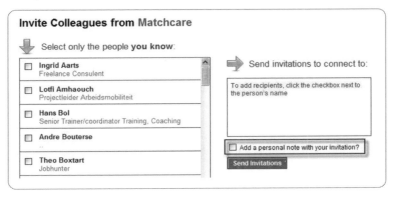

With the options of *Outlook, Webmail, Colleagues, Classmates* and *Invite Contacts* mentioned earlier, you can add a *Personal note,* which enables you to send out an invitation to a group of people (see screenshot); we strongly recommend using this.

For example:

> Dear (ex-) colleague,
>
> I have recently discovered LinkedIn and I would like to connect with you.
> Looking forward to hearing from you!
>
> Regards,
> John Doe
>
> N.B. If you would rather not connect with me, please click on *Archive* and not on *I don't know you.*

The above example contains 244 characters. Make allowances for the fact that an invitation message cannot contain more than 256 characters (including spaces).

I don't know you

If more than five of the people you have invited to join your network specify that they do not know you (by responding to your request with *I don't know you*), your opportunities to easily invite people to connect with you will be restricted by LinkedIn. This is because LinkedIn wants you to make strong connections and not to send out invitations at random; these can be perceived by some as undesirable messages, i.e. spam. If you do not know someone personally and want to connect with them, we recommend that you send them an InMail first. If your LinkedIn account is blocked, the only thing you can do is send an e-mail to Customer Service (option available at the bottom of your home page) explaining why, and requesting them to unblock you. This will be successful in most cases, but try not to let it come to that point.

Individual invitation

→ **Send InMail**

→ **Add John to your network**

→ Forward this profile to a connection

To the right of the profile you can see: *Add John to your network*. If you click here, you will see the following two screens:

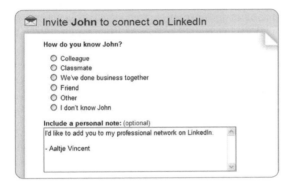

The moment you invite someone individually, you have to indicate how you know this person. You will be offered a drop-down menu including all your jobs and courses; select the appropriate one.

5.7 ACCEPTING INVITATIONS

Now that you are actively participating on LinkedIn, you will also start receiving invitations to link with people. You can accept invitations by clicking on the yellow *Accept* button. Some Frequently Asked Questions are:

1. *What do I do with invitations I do not want to accept?*
   Click on the *Archive* button and the person who sent you the invitation will not be notified. It may well be the case later on though that this person will think: 'Hey, I did not get a response from so and so…'

2. *What do I do with invitations from people I don't know?*
You can send them a *Reply* first, for example, asking them to specify how you know each other.
3. *What do I do with contacts I no longer wish to be connected to?*
Delete contacts via *Contacts-My Connections* in the top column on your home page, and then on the right, the option *Remove Connections;* tick the box and delete. Your contact will *not* be notified about this.

Important: It may be the case that over the years you have used various e-mail addresses or that you are currently using several. For example: addresses under the previous name of your provider, various private e-mail addresses, and several work e-mail addresses. Anyone who has access to these e-mail addresses can invite you to become their LinkedIn contact via such an old or rarely used e-mail address. If LinkedIn has just one e-mail address of you in its records, then at the moment you accept this invitation – sent to an e-mail address that is unknown to LinkedIn – LinkedIn will ask you to create a new profile. Make sure that you DO NOT do this. Continue working with the one profile you already have.

You can resolve this issue by adding more e-mail addresses via *Settings* (on the upper right-hand corner), going to the section *Email Addresses,* and within that *Add email address.* In this way, people can invite you by using any of your e-mail addresses, without LinkedIn automatically asking you to create a new profile.

It may be the case that you have more than one profile on LinkedIn without realizing it. Unfortunately this happens frequently. You can check whether you have one or more profiles on LinkedIn by typing your name in *Search People.* If you are listed with more than one profile, you will have to delete the other profiles (see page 97).

N.B. The 'old' e-mail addresses do need to be active. In other words, you must have access to them so that LinkedIn can confirm that they are valid e-mail addresses.

5.8 LINKEDIN ANSWERS

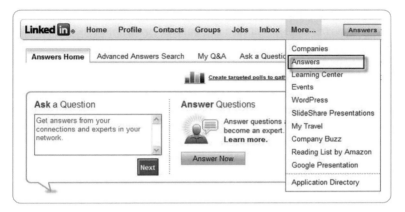

If you are looking for new work, you will regularly have questions like:

- Who can tell me more about the career counsellor course at institute X?
- Which agency should I approach for freelance/interim assignments in the childcare sector?
- What is the culture of company XYZ like? What do trainees think of their training programme?
- What is it like making the switch from a big organization to a small company?
- What experiences do other people have with applying for a job at company XYZ?
- Which recruitment and selection agencies are specialized in personal assistant vacancies?
- Who knows an innovative trainer in conducting job interviews?
- Who can advise me on making the switch from being an IT employee to becoming an independent IT consultant?

Do you have a business question like the ones above? Then confront your network with your question, and you will often get a rapid response. Through *Answers* in the main menu under the option *More...*, users can

ask questions that can be answered by everyone on LinkedIn.
If you want, you can limit the visibility of the question to a maximum of 200 first-degree connections. This feature is intended to promote discussion and exchange of information. The major benefit of this tool is that it enables you to reach a big group of direct contacts and start a discussion with them. This often produces innovative and surprising insights and answers. People like to be seen as an authority in their field. If you approach people in this way, they are usually willing to think along with you and call or e-mail back with information. The reward for the persons answering the question lies in the fact that they can demonstrate their expertise on the *Questions & Answers* forum. We need to stress that it is formally not allowed to advertise via *Answers*, to pose improper questions, or to repeat a question that has already been placed. You are allowed to ask ten questions a month.

You can ask your question directly to up to 200 first-degree connections. They will receive your question in their standard mailbox. This LinkedIn option is therefore ideally suited to asking a question to many people simultaneously; everyone you ask the question to, will then be made aware of what you are involved in at that moment. So think carefully about what impact a question will have on your activities and profiling in your search for new work. Because the question you are asking can by default be seen by everyone on LinkedIn, it is more or less expected that you phrase the question in English.

Earn expertise

If a star appears in a profile, this tells you that this person has proven their expertise by answering questions. By doing this, the person gains status and reputation within LinkedIn; which always gets noticed by recruiters! The person asking the question can choose the best answer, and in doing this, award the provider of the answer an expertise point, as long as the answer has been given publicly.

Reward expertise

Conversely, if you have asked a question on a forum, you yourself can reward someone's expertise by letting them know this. The four steps to do this are as follows:

1. Click on the *More... – Answers* tab and the section *My Q&A.*
2. Then click on *Rate Answers* next to the relevant question.
3. Next select the box *Good.*
4. Confirm this choice by clicking on *Rate.*

Re-opening a question

As this function is rather hidden away, here is a useful tip if you wish to re-open a question. Click on the *More... – Answers* tab and then on *My Q&A.* Then search for the question you wish to re-open and click on it (hyperlink). To the left of this question you will find a link *Re-open this question to answers.* By doing this, you are asking the question again and you can then send it to another 200 (new) contacts.

Go back to My Questions | Next »

Question expired **3 months ago.**
* Completely hide question
* Re-open this question to answers
   Rate Answers

Does your company have a social media protocol?

I'm looking for examples or guidelines of corporate social media protocols for employees.

Does you company have a social media protocol for sites such as Blogs, LinkedIn, Facebook or Twitter?

posted 4 months ago in **Personnel Policies** | Closed

6. Applying for jobs and LinkedIn

6.1 WHERE DO YOU WANT TO WORK?

You have now taken the following steps in career management via LinkedIn:

- Your profile: your public CV and testimonial.
- Your update, newsletter or 'microblog'.
- Your contacts: finding and inviting them.

If everything has gone well, you are now fully active on LinkedIn. You have taken the following steps: your profile is optimally fine-tuned, you are sending updates at regular intervals, and your contacts are being adequately informed about your professional development. We will now proceed to (the section) 'your job market' : where do you want to work, and who are the recruiters?

When you start looking for new work, a special job market exists where you will be most effective and successful. In other words, you have your own 'personal labour market' within the bigger labour market. In job hunting terms, we call this your *target group*. The question is: where would you like to work? Chart all the companies or organizations that you would really like to work for, and that are located within the maximum travelling distance you are prepared to travel – whether by car, bike or public transport. This is a very important step. It is not relevant whether there are any vacancies there at the moment; what is relevant is that you are now going to network in a focussed manner.

LinkedIn plays an essential role in the process of charting your labour market. On LinkedIn you will find thousands of company profiles (*Companies*). According to an American study carried out by *BusinessWeek*, LinkedIn is now the favourite location for jobseekers to find more information about a (potential) employer. A company profile is available as soon as you click on a company name when you read someone's profile. Additionally, using *Companies Search* gives you quick and direct access to the organizations/companies that are relevant for you. Our advice is to use the *Companies Search* function intensively:

On the *Company* profiles, as in the above Greenpeace example, you will find the employees of every company, whether they are part of your own network or not, and also information on which contacts you can approach them through. After all, the people who are currently doing the work you want to do in the future will be the first to hear about any such vacancy!

You can also search for the profiles of hiring managers (the ones who are looking for a new member of staff) and recruiters and find out directly which of your contacts knows them already. If they have ticked the *Job Inquiries* box in their *Contact Settings*, this is a confirmation that they are open to being approached by active jobseekers. This means that you can simply call them to discuss the possible mutual benefits.

From all these millions of profiles, LinkedIn distils a summary for you, of all the information that could be useful to you:

- All the employees of the appropriate company who are in your personal network, ranked according to the strength of the connection (up to and including the third degree)
- An overview of new employees and ex-employees
- Recent promotions within the company
- Popular profiles, for example of people who were recently in the news, who are mentioned in blogs, who take part in groups and/or who appear frequently in the search results or activities of the LinkedIn network. These personal profiles are the ones that are read most often on LinkedIn!
- A list of companies where most employees worked *prior to* joining the present company
- A list of companies which most employees *go to* after leaving this company
- An overview of companies with which the most employees are connected
- Financial data and public business information, such as number of employees and website address (if available)
- Advertised jobs on LinkedIn

At the same time, there are many interesting trends to be found related to the LinkedIn users of the relevant company, such as:

- The locations/regions where most of the employees live
- The most occurring job titles, expressed in percentages
- List of schools and universities where most of the employees have studied
- Average age, and the ratio of men/women.
- How long on average people stay at the company, and when they graduated

Companies with a company account on LinkedIn have a separate *Careers* tab, under which more dynamic information can be found, such as:

- Specific recruitment messages where content is modified dynamically to suit the requirements of the page visitor, based

on industry, position, location and seniority. For example, engineers see specific content that is applicable to them, while sales professionals will see other messages and information
- Testimonials from employees (*Employee Spotlight*)
- Integration of the LinkedIn Polls module for more interaction with visitors
- Video clips to give a taste of the company culture
- *Recruiter Profiles* so that potential candidates know who they can contact
- An overview of vacancies at the company that are advertised via LinkedIn
- Links to the own corporate career site

This 'personal job market analysis' produces interesting and often crucial data that can be important in finding new work.

6.2 YOUR INTERMEDIARIES

Every job market has its own specific intermediaries, such as recruitment and selection agencies, headhunters, recruitment agencies, temporary staffing agencies and agencies for freelancers and contractors. Recruiters from these agencies are extremely active on LinkedIn and have their own profile. It is advisable to approach them, if possible by phone, and to make them your LinkedIn contacts.

....

TIP: Recruiters also make vacancies known via their own updates, so keep a constant eye out for these!

....

You can access the intermediaries that are relevant for you in two ways:

1. By making a phone call to the personnel or recruitment department of the companies where you want to work, and asking them the following three questions:
   a. How do you deal with vacancies in the field of...?

b. What is the name of the manager of department X?
c. Which temporary job agency, secondment agency or recruitment and selection agency does your company work with?
2. *Advanced People Search* (also see page 74) for finding individual connections.

Using the *Advanced* option, you can carry out a search on company name and on *hiring managers*:

Within the LinkedIn network, you can fine-tune your search further around a post code and industry.

Hiring managers and their recruiters use LinkedIn for:

1. Informal recruiting. They ask current employees for appropriate profiles of their contacts.
   As we mentioned earlier, this is the most important source of recruiting new employees. Colleagues can now say: 'Oh, I know a good candidate, just look up her LinkedIn profile.'
2. By viewing the profiles of the contacts of their own employees directly or (assuming that current employees have contacts from their trade associations or classmates in their profiles, for example) viewing 'contacts of the contacts'.

6.3 JOBS/VACANCIES

As you will have gathered by now: LinkedIn is strongly career-oriented. So of course it has a vacancy section. *LinkedIn Jobs* is located in the upper menu.

Use *LinkedIn Jobs* to search for vacancies, view them, and you will be able to see immediately which of your contacts can help you get the job you are after. LinkedIn considers this aspect of great importance, and this can be seen in almost all the communication that the company issues to the outside world or offers to the users and recruiters. Think of the advertising options for companies and the search functions that have been built in. In this way, LinkedIn supports both the jobseeker and the employer in matching employment supply with demand.

There are five options available via *LinkedIn Jobs*, four of which are only accessible to employers. The *Advanced Job Search* option is especially designed for you, the jobseeker. Clicking this option will result in a search window being displayed, in which a large number of options are available to help you fine-tune your search for vacancies.

The way in which jobs can be searched on LinkedIn is not very different from how they can be found on popular job boards. You can carry out searches on keywords, and fine-tune the search results according to location, position level, how long the vacancy has been open, job title, company, area of expertise, or industry. The following is a short description of all the options available, including some search tips.

Simple search

In the search field (*Search for*), enter the search words that are most likely to be used in the texts of the job vacancies you are looking for. Make sure you use several options, such as synonyms, and English terms rather than terms in your native language. If your search produces no results initially, it does not necessarily mean that such a vacancy has not been advertised! It could simply be that the vacancy is described in text which is different from the search words you used. Using the search field you can search the *whole* vacancy, not just the vacancy text, but other fields like location and company names as well. So be as creative as you can in choosing your search terms.

Here is an example to help you: When you perform your search the dropdown list only allows you to select one country. Using keywords, you can enter the names of several countries, and this might produce the required result. For example, if you want to search the Benelux countries, type in: 'Netherlands OR Belgium OR Luxemburg'. Here you are making use of the special types of search available, the so-called *Boolean operators* (see page 88).

Fine-tuning your search

The following options will help you fine-tune your search:

- *Location*: Limit your search to jobs within a specific area or country. To search in a specific area, simply enter a post code and a search radius (distance)
- *Experience level*: Choose an appropriate level of experience
- *Search jobs posted*: Limit the search to vacancies posted within a certain period. Choosing a longer period will give an insight into the trends in the vacancies for these positions. You can also

make use of *Boolean operators* (see below)
- *Job Title*: Limit the search to specific job titles. It is possible to make use of *Boolean operators*
- *Company*: Limit the search to specific companies. It is possible to make use of *Boolean operators*
- *Job Function*: Limit the search to one or more job functions or areas of expertise. Use Ctrl-click (on Windows) or Cmd-click (on the Macintosh) to select more than one job function
- *Industry*: Limit the search to jobs in one or more industries. Use Ctrl-click (on Windows) or Cmd-click (on Macintosh) to select more than one industry

Sorting results

When sorting results (*Sort search results by*), you can use four criteria:

- When posted: Show the most recently posted vacancy first
- Location: Show the jobs in alphabetical order by location
- Company: Show the jobs in alphabetical order of company names
- Function: Show the jobs in alphabetical order of job titles

Special types of searches (*Boolean operators*)

As in many job boards, you can search in LinkedIn for vacancies in different ways. You can use keywords and *Boolean operators*, or more advanced searches so that a more restricted selection can be made on various fields.

Boolean operators improve the results by enabling you to specify more accurately what you are looking for and not looking for. This specific method of looking for information is named after George Boole (1815-1864). A variable is used, that can have only two values: true or false. The information required can therefore be more accurately described. Below are the Boolean operators as they are used in LinkedIn. The specified keywords are given as examples and can be replaced by other words. You can apply the Boolean operators in the free text fields of *Keywords*, *Job Title* or *Company*.

Boolean operators:

- 'Quoted' searches: If you are looking for an exact sentence, place the words between double quotation marks, for example: "product manager"
- - (minus sign) searches: If you are looking for a vacancy in which you wish to exclude a specific term, for example: sales, then use the minus sign. The search results will then not include any jobs with that term
- OR searches: If you are looking for a vacancy in which one or more terms occur, mention these terms separately, with the word OR (note the upper case) between the terms. For example: marketing OR advertising
- AND searches: If you are looking for a vacancy in which several terms occur, enter these terms separately with the word AND (note the upper case) in between. For example: manager AND finance, if you want to work as a finance manager
- Between brackets ( ) searches: If you want to perform a 'complex' search, for example, finding a job in marketing for advertising or sales, then you can combine the terms. For example: marketing AND (advertising OR sales). The results will be profiles in which the word marketing occurs in combination with advertising or sales

Vacancies: search results

The result of a search produces a list of jobs that meet your specified criteria, and that are advertised in the *LinkedIn Jobs* list. It goes without saying that you can apply directly to the jobs mentioned in the *LinkedIn Jobs* section. In addition to a cover note, you can add your contact data and a CV as an attachment to your application.

LinkedIn has a unique built-in option of allowing you to see directly whether you have any connections (direct or indirect) working at the company, advertising the job you are applying for. This means that you can approach them personally and ask them if they can introduce you. This way, your application will stand out more at the HRM department and you might have a contact who knows the hiring manager of this vacancy! Using a counter, LinkedIn shows how many connections can give you that introduction. As this raises the value of your application, we strongly recommend it. In any case, LinkedIn makes it very easy for you to use this option, so take advantage of it!

Please note that when there are no jobs matching your search criteria on *LinkedIn Jobs*, your search is automatically extended to the internet. This functionality is supported by 'Simply Hired'. Simply Hired contains millions of vacancies worldwide and is one of the biggest search sites for jobs. Simply Hired is a vertical search engine that searches a lot of different websites and job boards, such as Monster and Careerbuilder. You can view the jobs via LinkedIn and it will also show you who in your network or group works at the company (who advertises the job on the internet) and can help you get this job.

6.4 PREPARING FOR THE APPLICATION

Even if you see a job vacancy on a company site or a job board, you can still make excellent use of LinkedIn's options. It offers you a unique possibility of acquiring knowledge about:

1. The person named in the vacancy as the contact person
2. The person you have to address your letter of application to
3. The people who will actually be interviewing you

For all these people that you may call, write or speak to about the vacancy, you can find out beforehand:

- What position they currently have, and which positions they had prior to their current one
- Who they know and whether you have connections in common
- Whether you have taken the same courses
- The groups they are members of, and what messages they have written in their *updates*

This way, you will have more self-confidence when going for the interview. You can make a good impression right from the start and initiate an interesting discussion that goes deeper than the traffic or the weather!

TIP: If you want to have a profile 'at hand', you can mark it or print it in a number of ways. You can find these options to the right of the profile.

Including LinkedIn in your standard CV

If you are applying for a job, you can include a link to your LinkedIn profile in your CV which you have developed in Word format; this way you are letting people know 'who you are and who is recommending you'.
An example:

Curriculum Vitae
John Doe
Central Park 1225, 1000 AA New York
Date of birth: 7 May 1982
Contact: 212-12345678, johndoe@yahoo.net

http://www.linkedin.com/in/johndoe

LinkedIn in your e-mail signature

You can use your LinkedIn profile in your e-mail signature as well:

http://www.linkedin.com/in/johndoe

We will explain how to do this in more detail later (see page 99).

6.5   CONTACTING LINKEDIN USERS

InMail is the most effective way of communicating with other LinkedIn users for two reasons:

1. It is sent to the person's 'standard' e-mail address, so it comes straight into the mailbox of the person you are sending it to, and then that person can click on the link to arrive straight at your profile.
2. The message appears at the top of the home page of the person you are sending it to, and it stays there until the person responds to it.

The chance that your InMail will be read is therefore extremely high. Sending InMail to a first-degree contact is free. If you want to send an In-Mail to anyone further than a first-degree contact, you will need to have a paid subscription. But you can also make use of other options:

- Direct contact through a *LinkedIn Group*; send an InMail to your fellow group members. This is free of charge.
- Send an e-mail. An e-mail address will often be mentioned in the profile.
- If you can see the company someone works for, the e-mail address is usually structured in a logical way, like firstname.surname@companyname.com, and variations of this; try out a few combinations.
- Try to get an introduction via your personal network on LinkedIn (informal contact). It goes without saying that this option is highly recommended if there is already a 'strong' connection between you and the contact. This is what LinkedIn likes to see! However, this option is not very effective if there are several links in the chain.
- Call the person up! This has proven to be the most effective method, because you will get far more information and you can respond to it directly. An e-mail can come across as cold and distant. Go to the company's website to find the relevant telephone number, or look it up in the online telephone books.

The message you send has to be clear and focussed. That starts with the subject line, so that the person actually opens your e-mail. Some tips on how to set up a first e-mail:

- The message is about the person and not about you as a job-seeker. The person is the focus not the transaction, so put yourself in that person's shoes and make the message personal.
- The opening sentences have to make the reason you are approaching this person clear. Anything else you mention distracts from the main message. You have just one chance to make a good first impression.
- Approach the person as an equal; you are engaging in professional communication.
- If you want to get in touch with someone with a view to finding new work, mention this explicitly.
- Make your message clear. Keep it short, relevant and be enthusiastic!
- Make sure that you specify an action you wish the other person to take. End your mail by specifying this, and make sure it stands out from the rest of the text. You want that person to reply, after all.
- Do not forget to specify all your contact details, and to refer to additional information the person can access directly. You have to make it as easy as possible for them to respond.

6.6 TIME INVESTMENT

We often hear the comment: 'Keeping up-to-date on LinkedIn costs (too) much time!' Yes, engaging with LinkedIn costs time. Serious users spend some time every day on maintaining their profile, or at the very least reading all their messages. Your LinkedIn home page is the portal for this. You can modify everything on that page and also follow the modification and new connections of your own contacts. In our experience, this investment is well worth the effort. The power of your LinkedIn activity lies most in the long-term relationships that you can engage in and maintain in this way. LinkedIn is a fantastic, time-saving tool (in the long

run) for remaining in the frame as a professional, now, and for the rest of
your working life.

....

TIP: If you want to follow your first-degree contacts very
efficiently, you can do this in two ways: via RSS or via the
Status Update page *See more updates*, that you can then
bookmark as one of your favourites on the internet.

....

7. LinkedIn for advanced users

7.1 EXTRAS FOR YOUR BASIC PROFILE

If you have taken all the steps we have outlined up till now, you already have an excellent start for orientating, networking, applying for jobs, and getting information on LinkedIn:

- Your profile – your public CV and testimonial – is complete and up-to-date.
- You are maintaining your update, newsletter or 'microblog'.
- Your contacts know where to find you and you know where to find them, and you continue to work on your 'network mainte-nance'.
- You are charting your job market (where you want to work and which recruiters you are interested in) using LinkedIn.
- Your CV and your e-mail signature include a link to your LinkedIn profile.
- You are preparing thoroughly for your job interviews using LinkedIn.

Once you start working with LinkedIn more intensively and actively, you will want to make use of the many extra options it offers for your profile, your 'personal branding strategy', or for networking. You will come up against problems, and you will regularly have questions you want answered. We will go into all these extras in more detail in this chapter.

7.1.1 Extracting your CV

If you have your CV in Word format and you are completely happy with it, in other words, it describes you and your qualities fully and is geared towards the position you are looking for, LinkedIn offers you the possibility to import this information with a couple of mouse clicks. If your CV lacks this quality, we advise you to take some time to build up your profile manually.

A CV extraction goes like this:

- On the top of your screen, click on *Profile*
- On the right of your screen click on *Import your résumé*
- Click on Browse, find your CV and click on *Upload Résumé*

Please note: In our experience, this option does not always work flawlessly, for example, if your CV has a layout that LinkedIn does not recognize, or if it contains photos and images. The only solution then is to copy and paste text from your Word document onto your LinkedIn profile.

7.1.2 Multiple language profiles

LinkedIn's primary profile interface in most countries will be in the English language. But LinkedIn offers the possibility of viewing the interface in another language; see *Language* option in the menu bar at the bottom. You can change all terms, fields and (default) text messages into the language of your choice. The profiles that are made in these languages are also fully indexed; in other words, they can be found if the appropriate *Search* options are used. Users who choose one of these languages for the LinkedIn interface by default, will see their French, German, Italian, Portugese or Spanish language profile first. See for yourself: on your own profile page, click on Spanish and you will see that all the LinkedIn basics are in Spanish. If it is a useful career move for you to have a Spanish language profile, we advise you to create this as a second profile.

LinkedIn offers you the possibility of creating a second profile in almost any language you want, for example in Dutch or Danish. Profiles in languages other than German, French, Italian, Portugese and Spanish however, are not being indexed at the moment (in other words, they will not be found via the *Search* options). The value of such a Dutch or Danish language profile is therefore extremely limited at the moment. However, it can be relevant for you to make a profile in that language, for example, for business relations from Denmark who want to view your profile. Even a third or fourth profile in another language is an option. In the future, it is expected that LinkedIn will fully support the profiles in the other languages via *Search*.

Using the option *Edit my profile*, it is possible to create several LinkedIn profiles in more than forty different languages. In the next screen, you can choose your language and use another *headline*. After performing this step, a new profile will be created, including many elements that have been re-used from your primary profile. Now it is simply a matter of translating the profile and making it complete. LinkedIn makes this task easy for you by showing you the text from your primary profile.

TIP: Long texts can be translated quickly via websites like http://translate.google.com.

7.1.3 Double profiles of yourself

It may happen that you have more than one profile (*user account*) on LinkedIn, without being aware of it. Therefore, we advise you to type your name into the *Search People* window. Your own profile or profiles will automatically appear in the search results. If more than one profile exists, all you can do is choose which ones you want to delete, and to re-invite all the contacts you had linked to that profile to the remaining undeleted profile. You can delete a redundant profile yourself:

1. Find out under which e-mail address and password you created the profile.
2. If you are logged on to the 'right' LinkedIn profile, log out by clicking on *Sign out* in the top right-hand corner.
3. The following text will appear: *You are now signed out*. Click on *Sign in again*.
4. Log on with the e-mail address and password that correspond to the profile you wish to delete. If you cannot remember your password, click on *Forgot Password* and you can request a new password for every registered e-mail address of that account.

5. Click on *Settings* in the top right-hand corner of the page.
6. Click on *Close your account* in the right-hand column.
7. Select *Duplicate account* as the reason for deleting it.
8. Click on *Continue*.
9. Click on *Verify account*. You can add the e-mail addresses that were linked to your deleted profile to your 'right' account/profile on LinkedIn (after 24 hours).

You can find more information about the importance of adding your old and active e-mail addresses to your only and correct profile on page 72.

Unfortunately, it is not possible to merge two separate accounts. The only option is to delete the duplicate account, notify the contacts you have on this account via your valid profile, and re-invite them immediately as connections on your other account.

N.B. If you cannot remember which *login* you used to create the unwanted profile, you can ask the LinkedIn customer service to delete it for you (see page 121).

7.1.4 Specifying former/maiden name

It may be the case that you are married and that you now have a LinkedIn profile under the name of your partner.

Then LinkedIn offers you the possibility to specify your original surname. You can do this via the option *Edit My Profile*; next to your name, click on *Edit*. You will be given the option to fill in your *Former/Maiden Name* and make this visible to your first-degree connections, your personal network (first- and second-degree), or everybody. The advantage of this addition to your contact data is that you can be found by former class- and college mates who may more often use your original surname in their searches. For example: Anna Johnson's surname before she married was Mulder. If she defines this in LinkedIn and also ticks the box indicating that she wishes to be found by everyone, she can still be found if someone searches for 'Anna Mulder'.

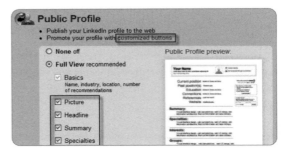

7.1.5 Promoting your public profile

New LinkedIn users often wonder to what extent information on LinkedIn is confidential or private. It is possible to not or only partly make your LinkedIn account visible publicly. You can find the settings for this under *Settings – Public Profile*.

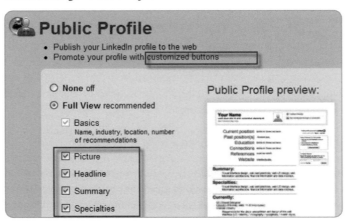

This is where you can specify what Google or other search engines can allow others to see on your public profile, like your photo, headline or summary. Your own first-degree contacts, and your second- and third-degree contacts can always see your whole profile; this is rather stating the obvious since that is how LinkedIn has been designed.

A truly valuable extra option is promoting your public profile with *Customized buttons*: http://www.linkedin.com/profile?promoteprofile=.

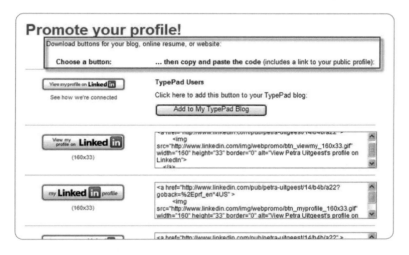

This enables you to make your own website, your blog, your online CV or standard CV much more valuable by directing your reader to your LinkedIn profile with one mouse click! There is a wide range of LinkedIn logos available. Choose the logo that is most appropriate for the subject you wish to use it for; for example, a larger logo for your own website, and a smaller one for your e-mail signature.

7.1.6 Modifying, moving or deleting a recommendation

At some point in your career, it may happen that you want to modify, move, or delete a recommendation. You may want to emphasize other talents, or you want to make (or have made) a career switch, or you may want to delete a work experience/study from your profile altogether.

You can modify your recommendations under the options *Profile – Recommendations* in the main menu. To manage your recommendations, do the following:

- Click on *Profile – Recommendations* in the main menu.
- Search the recommendations you want to manage and click on *Manage* next to the corresponding recommendation.

- The above screen will be displayed. You can personalize all the text fields, including the recommendation itself. Then you can ask the person who wrote the recommendation to modify it, or ask them to approve a modification you have made yourself. You will have the opportunity of viewing the 'new' recommendation, so that you can approve or reject it again before posting it. If you are still not satisfied with it and how well it represents you, you can ask for another version.
- To delete a recommendation, we advise you to simply call the contact or send them an InMail with the request and an explanation.

- If you wish to retract/delete a recommendation that you have given to someone else, click on: *Looking for recommendations you've made? Click here,* and then, for example: 'John Doe as Graphic/ Web Designer'. Then click on *Withdraw this recommendation* and then on *Send.* Note: The person to whom you originally gave the recommendation will not be notified about this by LinkedIn.

7.2 MAKING YOUR PROFILE MORE ATTRACTIVE

Perhaps you have already noticed this in other people's profiles; there are a lot of options available to help you make your basic profile more attractive. This gives you even more opportunities to highlight your talents using your profile, and it further supports your 'personal branding strategy'. You can import applications to your LinkedIn profile to help you.

TIP: We strongly advise you to make use of the options outlined here. It is very important to put yourself firmly in the spotlight, and to stand out from the many other candidates looking for new work and assignments.

You can find the extra applications in the top menu under *More... – Application Directory.* These applications can either help you raise your profile on LinkedIn, or provide added benefits from your participation on LinkedIn. In this section, we will go into more detail about the most important applications that can help improve your profile:

- Google Presentation
- WordPress or Bloglink
- SlideShare presentations
- Reading List by Amazon
- MyTravel
- Events

We will guide you through the first steps in using these applications. An important thing to remember is that if you use an application that affects your profile on LinkedIn, all your first-degree contacts will be notified immediately!

If they regularly visit their home page (we recommend that you visit yours at least once a day), they will see your new and unique upload straight away! You can modify this setting separately for each application.

7.2.1 Google Presentation

Google Presentation enables you to share all your know-how and expertise via LinkedIn through, for example, PowerPoint presentations you have used for your team, for the management team, in a training course, or for your Board of Directors. Please note that you need to create or setup a Google-account in order to be able to use this application; check http://docs.google.com.

Just follow these steps:

- Click on *More...* – *Application Directory* and select *Google Presentation*.
- Tick the checkbox *Display on my profile* and, optionally, *Display on LinkedIn homepage*, and then click on *Add application*.
- Now click on *Sign in*.
- Next click on *New* to create a new presentation, or click on *Upload* for an existing presentation.
- Go back to your LinkedIn home page *Google Docs* and tick the checkbox on *Update settings*, etc.

Posting a video film on your profile

You can also post a film of your own or someone else on your profile. Adding moving images and sound will make you stand out even more. Follow these steps:

- First post your film on YouTube.
- Follow the steps given earlier to log on to Google Presentation to add your film.
- Click on *Insert* and then on *Video*.

- Find the film you are looking for on YouTube, click on *Select video*, and give it a name.
- Now click on *Save & Close*.
- Go back to LinkedIn and click on *Sign in to access and upload your presentations*, etc.

7.2.2 WordPress blog

WordPress enables you to post your own blog on LinkedIn. Personal branding specialists recommend that you update your blog at least once a week. If you want to stand out as the right candidate for new work, a blog is an excellent way of presenting yourself professionally. Just follow these steps:

- Click on *More... – Application Directory* in the main menu and select *WordPress*.
- Tick the checkbox *Display on my profile* and, optionally, *Display on LinkedIn homepage* and then click on *Add application*.
- Click on: *Your WordPress blog* URL, and create an account via *Sign up now*, with a user name, password and your e-mail address. Make sure that the checkbox next to *Gimme a blog! (Like username.wordpress.com)* is ticked.
- Modify the blog title if necessary, choose your language, and *Sign up!*
- Once your account has been activated, make an entry using the option *New post*.

You have now imported your own blog!

7.2.3 SlideShare presentations

With SlideShare, you can post your PowerPoint presentations, PDF documents, or even YouTube films of your presentation or workshops on your profile. Just follow these steps:

- Click on *More... – Application Directory* in the main menu and select *SlideShare Presentations*.
- Tick the checkbox *Display on my profile* and, optionally, *Display on LinkedIn homepage* and then click on *Add application*.

- First create an account via *Create and link SlideShare account now* with a user name, your e-mail address and your password.
- Select *Browse and select files now.*
- Your first-degree contacts will be notified about your upload! As mentioned earlier, if they regularly visit their home page (which we already recommended you do at least once a day), they will see your upload straight away!
- Give your document an appropriate title and *Publish!*
- The document will appear on your profile. LinkedIn also offers you the possibility of immediately notifying selected contacts via InMail.

7.2.4 Reading list by Amazon

Using this application, LinkedIn offers you the possibility of informing your contacts about the literature you are reading at the moment or have read in the past; this is an ideal way to let others know that you are completely up-to-date with developments in your areas of expertise! If you are up-to-date on your reading list, your contacts will see at once that you are the person they need to get in touch with for the latest information and insights. The only restriction is that the book should be available on Amazon.

Just follow these steps:

- Click on *More... – Application Directory* in the main menu and select *Reading List by Amazon.*
- Tick the checkbox *Display on my profile* and, optionally, *Display on LinkedIn homepage* and then click on *Add application.*
- Type in the title of a book in the section: *Find a book to add to your reading list.*
- Choose one of the three options: I want to read it, I am reading it now, or I already read it.
- You have the option of mentioning why the book appeals to you. Now click on *Save.*

7.2.5 MyTravel

If you decide to use MyTravel, this means that your travel plans contain relevant information for your first-degree contacts. If you are a purchaser and you travel all over the world, this might be relevant; it shows insights that you, for example, do your purchasing in China and India. It can also happen that your contact is in New York at the same time as you are, and that can lead to an unexpected dinner date together! In our experience, if you make use of MyTravel for short-distance trips in your own country, your travel messages may be regarded as redundant and therefore annoying information. So think carefully about whether this application adds value to your profile in terms of finding new work. Follow these steps if you believe the application will help further your work interests:

- Click on *More...* – *Application Directory* in the main menu and select *MyTravel*.
- Tick the checkbox *Display on my profile* and, optionally, *Display on LinkedIn homepage* and then click on *Add application*.
- Create an account via *Do you have a TripIt account?* Tick the checkbox *No, I want to sign up*. Do this by specifying your e-mail address and home city.
- It is also possible to follow the travel plans of ten of your contacts.
- Activate your account and share your travel plans!

7.2.6 LinkedIn Events

LinkedIn Events is the application that is always available under *More...* – *Application Directory* in the main menu.

Including events in your profile is an outstanding way of letting others know which events you are visiting or planning to visit, or even organizing yourself. It gives your contacts and readers of your profile – as with all the other profiling applications – an up-to-date picture of how you keep up with developments in your area of expertise, of the congresses, training courses or workshops you organize, and where you give presentations.

The application also allows you to search for events taking place all over the world by time and location. If you specify that you are visiting an event, this event will appear on your profile.

An example:

You can also add your own event via *Add an Event*. The following screen will then be displayed:

Add an Event

* Event Title:	[ ]
* Date & Time:	[08/02/2009] [🗓] [8:00am] to [08/02/2009] [🗓] [5:00pm]
	☐ This is a virtual event.
Venue Name:	[ ]
	Ex. "Carnegie Hall"
Location:	[ ]
	Ex. "881 7th Ave. New York, NY 10019"
Website:	[http://]

Are you attending? ○ I'm attending   ◉ I'm interested   ○ I'm not attending

Are you organizing? ☐ Yes, I am organizing this event.

➕ Add more details

[Publish Event] [Preview Event] [Save Draft] or Cancel

In the *Add more details* field you can add extra information!
Fill in all the details. Note: The elements *I'm attending, Attendee* and *Publish Event* will now be visible on your profile. In addition, LinkedIn also offers the possibility of informing your contacts about the event directly via an InMail.

7.2.7 Other applications
LinkedIn also has a couple of other applications for you, however in the context of career management, these are not so relevant for raising your profile. But it is possible that you will benefit from them, so we will describe them briefly here. Advanced LinkedIn users will not need any specific instructions about how to use them.

LinkedIn Polls
You can use this application for market research using LinkedIn input.

LinkedIn Buzz
You can use this application for monitoring messages on Twitter using keywords of your choice, for example about companies, job vacancies, etc.

7.3 MAKING OPTIMAL USE OF YOUR ONLINE NETWORK

7.3.1 Address book

Just like any other online or physical address book, LinkedIn offers you the possibility of linking telephone numbers, e-mail addresses, meetings and other notes, to your individual contacts. This has made LinkedIn an online address book that you have permanent access to as long as you are connected to the internet.

Access the address book via *Contacts – Connections*, and select a contact. Click on *Edit details*, and you can start filling your address book as is shown in the example on the next page.

Edit Contact BETA

Jacco Valkenburg

Title:	Writer / Author
Company:	Recruitment via LinkedIn & Solliciteren via LinkedIn
Email:	j⋅ ⋅⋅⋅⋅ ⋅.nl primary
	Add
Phone:	▭ ▾ 06-⋅⋅⋅⋅⋅⋅⋅⋅⋅
	Add
IM:	Add an Instant Message
Address:	Add an Address
Website:	www.iprc.nl
	Add
Birthday:	Add a Birthday
Other Info:	co-auteur: Solliciteren via LinkedIn
	Add
Notes:	adviseur Recruitment en Talentmanagement Oplossingen

7.3.2 Following a contact's activities

Your home page provides an overview of everything your first-degree contacts do on LinkedIn, their updates, the new contacts they have made, presentations, etc. We advise you to view your home page on a daily basis, even if it is for just a few minutes. Following the activities of your chosen contacts is one of the most valuable aspects of LinkedIn. It can produce all kinds of results; seeing who a contact has just connected with can lead to new work, or you can even simply follow what literature a contact is reading.

We often hear: 'But we get all these messages in our Outlook on e-mail!' This is true, but it is only a brief summary of all the new activities of your contacts on LinkedIn. We consider checking your home page every day a must, if you want to derive the maximum benefits from LinkedIn, so that you are in the picture for new work.

If you want to follow your first-degree network very easily, you can do this efficiently in two ways: via RSS (see below) and via the update collection site *See more updates*, which you can then mark as a favourite on the internet.

RSS stands for *Really Simple Syndication*. You can access RSS feeds of the updates of your first-degree connections, and of selected *Answers* categories.
Follow these steps:

• Click on the orange icon next to *Network Updates*:

• Select the options you want in the window that appears next:

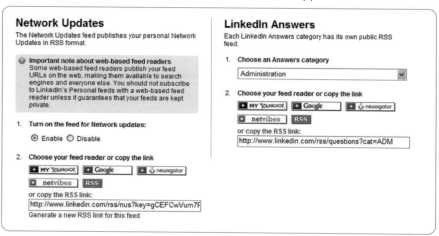

7.3.3 Mutual introductions

If you have built up a whole network of contacts on LinkedIn, you may now be thinking: 'Wouldn't it be a good idea for those two people to get in touch with each other?' Or: 'I would really like to be introduced to John

Doe.''In real life' you would do this via telephone or e-mail; we often introduce people to each other in this way. It is also possible to do this via
LinkedIn. The advantage of using LinkedIn for this purpose is that the profiles of the two people involved immediately become available. It is an option that is a bit hidden, and works like this:

To the right of the profile, and then:

And then:

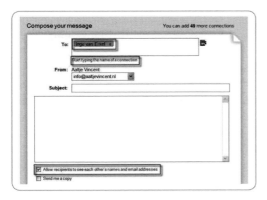

At IN, you choose the person you want to send the mail to, for example: to
Carla.
Write your text. Example:

Ron and Carla,

You don't know each other, but I think you'd benefit from meeting because you're both involved in educating young people in technology, but each from a different perspective (see your profiles).
Look forward to hearing how you get on.

Have a nice day
John

Do not forget to leave the checkbox ticked so that both can see each other's e-mail address.

7.3.4 Sending a message to more than one connection

You may at some point want to send a message to more than one connection. There are two ways of doing this. For messages to fifty connections or less, you can use the function *Compose Message/InMail* (see page 92). For messages to more than fifty connections, but less than 200, we advise you to use the *Answers* option. For using the *Answers* option to send a message, go to *Ask a Question* and tick the checkbox *Only share this question with connections I select* as the first step. You can make a selection based on geographic location, area of expertise and/or individuals.

7.3.5 Advertising via LinkedIn DirectAds

It is probably not the first thing that comes to mind when you think of LinkedIn, but you can also promote yourself as a freelancer or one-man business. This advertising possibility is located right at the bottom of the home page under *Advertising*; click here and you will be sent to the *Advertise With Us* page. Click on the *LinkedIn DirectAds link*. This option enables you to display small advertisements (*'banners'*) directly on the home pages of specific users.
You determine the content of the banner, such as the logo of your company or a passport photo (optional), three lines of advertising text, and the link to your website. Your name with a link to your LinkedIn profile is also visible on the banner. This banner will appear on the top right-hand cor-

ner of home pages of contacts you have selected as soon as they log on! You can define the target group via (maximum 3) criteria such as company size, job function, industry, seniority, gender, age, geography, etc. Users who do not meet the defined criteria will not see the banner. This certainly is an interesting option if you want to bring yourself to the attention of people outside your own field/connections.

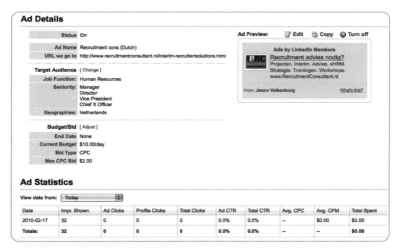

You do not need a huge budget to advertise on LinkedIn either. There are two options: payment per thousand displays: CPM (*Cost-Per-Mille*); or payment per click (CPC, *Cost-Per-Click*). You pay a fixed amount for one thousand banner displays or for every time someone clicks on a banner. With the CPC model, you pay only for the results; in other words for the number of times people click to visit your site. Both models allow you to determine a maximum budget per day. You can also determine the maximum cost price for a click on the advertising banner. In this way, you can avoid unpleasant surprises. A credit card payment is required, and a one-off payment of fifty dollars will be charged. This amount will be used for your first payments.

7.3.6 Finding anonymous profiles via Google
It can be handy to find out the names of anonymous search results on

LinkedIn. It will happen quite often that profiles displayed in search results, after a People Advanced Search, are outside your network. These
profiles outside your network are made anonymous, but contain keywords or combinations of keywords that are unique. If you type these keywords in your Google search, you will usually, though not always, be able
to find the profile with the full name of the person.
Follow these steps:

1. Use some of the unique keywords from the profile, such as a combination of education and previous employers.
2. Go to Google and type in: *site: www.linkedin.com [keywords]* and
   search. If you are searching in a specific country, for example The
   Netherlands (NL), you should use the search string *site:nl.linkedin.com
   [keywords]*

8. Reference: LinkedIn basics

8.1 LINKEDIN ELEMENTS

LinkedIn has an enormous range of possibilities. So allow us to take you on a tour of all the basic elements on your home page.

The central window

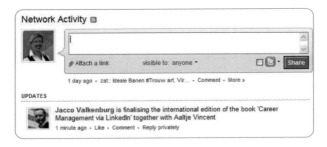

Inbox

Here you will see an overview of all InMails that you still have to take action on.

Update

Add a new update here (see page 54).

Status Update

This is where you can read the updates from all your first-degree connections, so you know what they are working on at the moment.

Connection update

This is where you can see who has recently made new contacts.

The main menu, top right-hand corner

People	This function enables you to perform an extensive search for people on LinkedIn (see page 73).
Jobs	This function is the entry point for finding vacancies published on LinkedIn (see page 85).
Answers	This option helps you ask questions or send messages to a large number of people simultaneously (see page 78).
Companies	This is the function for finding out everything regarding companies and their employees (see page 81).
Settings	This is where you can opt for a free account or a more comprehensive paid account. This is also the entry point for modifying various settings with regard to visibility, the messages you receive, etc.
Help	This is where you will find lots of answers to your questions (also see page 121 on Customer service).
Sign out	This is where you log off from your LinkedIn profile.

TIP: If you want to work on your profile on a colleague's computer for a few minutes and your colleague also has a LinkedIn account, she will first have to log off (via Sign out) before you can change your account data. Once you have finished, log off again so that your colleague can log on with her account data.

Language	This is where you can choose which language you want to work in, with the LinkedIn interface (see page 96).
Search options	There are six *Search* options, some of which have *Advanced* search features so that you can fine-tune your results:

Search People	Search for profiles using people's names
Search Jobs	Search on keywords for jobs, the *Advanced* option is definitely worth using here!
Search Companies	Search for companies on LinkedIn and find the people who are working there now.
Search Answers	If you are looking for a specific topic, you can enter a keyword here.
Search Inbox	You can search for a message you have received by entering a keyword that you know appears in the message.
Search Groups	By entering a keyword, you can find the group you are interested in.

TIP: Using *Search People*, you might come across the term *LinkedIn Network/Fellow group member*. This user is not connected to you, but you are members of the same *LinkedIn Group*. You can approach this person via a group introduction (InMail).

The main menu, top left-hand corner

Home
: Your home page is the starting page and appears as soon as you log on to LinkedIn.com. It is a crucial element of LinkedIn because the most important modifications and the most recent messages are displayed here.

Profile
: This leads you directly to your profile; you can view or modify your profile and manage your recommendations using this option.

Contacts –
My Connections
: Your address book containing your first-degree contacts can be found here.

This number indicates how many connections someone has. An orange circle indicates that the person has recently added new connections.

Imported Contacts
: This is where you can find people amongst your Outlook contacts who have not yet become your LinkedIn connections; you can invite them from here.

Profile Organizer
: Under this option you can see which profiles you have saved because you found them interesting.

Network Statistics
: Here you can see how many people you can approach directly in the first-, second- and third-degree via LinkedIn. Other general statistics about your LinkedIn profile can also be viewed.

Add Connections
: Using this option you can invite contacts to join your network, and you can also find ex-colleagues and former classmates.

Groups:
: This leads you straight to the discussion forums of your groups.

Inbox – Received
: This displays all the messages you have received.

Inbox – Sent
: This displays all the messages you have sent.

Inbox – Archived
: This displays all the messages you have archived.

Inbox – Compose
: Using this option, an InMail Message can be sent to a maximum of fifty people.

More... – Applications
: This shows the available LinkedIn applications, including the ones you use actively (see page 102).

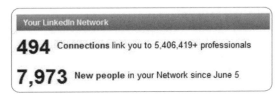

Here you can see immediately your number of connections and how many people you have added to your network.

On the home page, in the right-hand menu

People you may know. More about this feature on page 73.

Advertisement, one of LinkedIn's sources of income: this is a standard fixed element of your home page.

Who has viewed my profile? More on this on page 68.

Additionally, in the right-hand menu you will find the various applications (*widgets*, for people in the know) that you are using.

Bottom menu bar

Within the context of this book, we will go into more detail about three topics from the bottom menu bar. When you are an advanced user, we advise you to study the other topics yourself and explore whether they can be useful in promoting your work and profile.

N.B. We discussed *Advertising* (*LinkedIn DirectAds*) already (see page 113).

8.2 CUSTOMER SERVICE

This offers you the possibility of finding answers to Frequently Asked Questions via keywords. This section is only operational in English. Right at the top of this page, you can also access *LinkedIn Learning Centre*, the place to learn more about LinkedIn.

8.3 PAID MEMBERSHIP

When you participate on LinkedIn, you will have a standard, free account. Everything we have described in this book applies to the use of LinkedIn as an unpaid member:

- You can view the complete profile of your first-, second- and third-degree contacts.
- You can receive an unlimited number of InMails.
- You can send an unlimited number of messages to your first-degree contacts and your fellow-group members.
- At any given moment, you are allowed to have five outstanding introduction requests. An introduction request is a request to a contact of yours to be introduced to another contact (see page 64).
- With the six *Search* possibilities, you can receive three *alerts* per week.
- If you perform a search, you can receive a maximum of one hundred results per search.

If the above facilities are not enough for you, you can choose a more exclusive account, for which you pay extra. You will doubtless have noticed that LinkedIn reminds you of this premium account possibility at regular intervals.

There are three types of paid accounts. We will only describe the first type; for the other types, please see *Upgrade your account* or *Account & Settings*.

As of summer 2009, the first type of paid account costs 24.95 US dollars per month, or 249.50 US dollars per year. At the time of writing this book, this account stated to offer active users the following *extra* features:

- You can send three InMails per month to people who are not your first-degree contacts. If the person does not respond to your InMail within seven days, you are allowed to reuse this InMail within nine months.
- After your fifth saved *Search* you will get a weekly *alert*.
- At any given moment, you are allowed to have fifteen outstanding requests for introductions.
- When you perform a search, you will get a maximum of 300 results per search.
- *Open Link Network membership*: This means that you can send an unlimited number of messages to everyone who has a paid LinkedIn account.
- Customer Service answers your questions within one working day.
- You have access to an unlimited number of *reference searches* with one mouse click; recruiters use this to get a quick impression of who worked, or is working, in a specific period at a company (as your colleague).

8.4 TERMS OF USE

As a user you have to agree to the user agreement; most people just click on *I agree*. But the small print here is very important. Below is a list of the most important points to note, as there are a few things you are not allowed to do:

- Placing inappropriate information in fields that are not intended for this purpose. For example, it is not allowed to specify e-mail addresses, telephone numbers or number of connections in the name- or position fields.
- Placing information or initiating communication that is forbidden, slanderous, obscene or discriminatory, or that is liable to meet resistance in one way or another.
- Falsely stating or otherwise misrepresenting your identity, including but not limited to the use of a pseudonym, or misrepresenting your current or previous positions and qualifications, or your affiliations with a person or entity, past or present.

- Distributing any unsolicited or unauthorized advertising and promotional materials in the form of 'junk mail,' 'spam,' 'chain letters,' 'pyramid schemes,' or any other form of solicitation. This prohibition includes:
    a. Using LinkedIn invitations to send messages to people who don't know you;
    b. Using LinkedIn to connect to people who don't know you, and then send unsolicited promotional messages to those direct connections without their permission;
    c. Sending messages to distribution lists, newsgroup aliases, or group aliases.
- Stalking or harassing someone.
- Using LinkedIn for illegal purposes.
- Distributing information that is prohibited, for example confidential or secret information or material that is protected under copyright law.

About the authors

Aaltje Vincent

Aaltje Vincent is an experienced career coach, an authority in the field of job marketing, a coach and trainer for jobseekers and career coaches, operating under the name Aaltje Vincent & Company. Within her field, Aaltje's undivided passion lies in supporting and training people who, once they know what they are looking for, want to go out and find this new job. Over the last twenty years she has developed her own unique style of assisting people in this area: Job Marketing, an effective and creative way of approaching the job market. It is a method she applies in both individual and group outplacement, particularly for those who have not applied for a job in the past ten, twenty, or thirty years. She developed the training course 'Advanced Job Marketing for Career Coaches', and is a visiting lecturer at career coach courses. Additionally, she gives presentations and workshops on job marketing and career management via LinkedIn.

Her successful book, full of practical advice for jobseekers, *'Jobmarketing. Werk vinden, zo pak je het aan'* (Spectrum, 7th print run), was published in 2007.

http://www.linkedin.com/in/aaltjevincent and www.aaltjevincent.nl

Jacco Valkenburg

Jacco Valkenburg, born in 1971, is the founder of IPRC and Recruit2 and has been an independent recruitment expert, trainer and writer since 1996. With his extensive experience in the field of recruitment, he assists international organizations in improving their recruitment and selection processes, or even helps them by executing these processes. His success is based on clever application of new technologies, labour market communication, and years of expertise. IPRC is a provider of recruitment- and talent management solutions such as recruitment of individual specialists, setting up a project team for a specific purpose, or a fully operational recruitment team for, as an example, setting up a new enterprise.

Experience:
- Since 1996: Expert in international recruitment and selection of staff.
- Since 1999: Interim corporate recruiter/manager for Fortune 100 organizations.
- In 2003: Founded IPRC, recruitment consultancy services and project support.
- Since 2005: Experience with recruitment outsourcing/managed services.
- Since 2007: Blogger on various websites, including www.Global-RecruitingRoundtable.com
- In 2007: Started providing tailor-made training courses and workshops (www.RecruiterUniversity.eu).
- In 2008: Wrote *Recruitment via LinkedIn* (www.recruitmentvialinkedin.com).
- In 2009: Elected 'Best Social Recruiter'

www.Recruit2.com | www.RecruitmentviaLinkedin.com | www.RecruiterUniversity.eu

Update
Do you want to be kept up to date with all the developments in the field of 'career management via LinkedIn'? On the special website www.careermanagementvialinkedin.com you will find all the latest developments, training courses and workshops on this subject. For career coaches, work coaches, reintegration consultants, customer managers, and for everyone who helps people at the crossroads of their careers, there is an open network group on LinkedIn: Loopbaanprofessionals en carrièrecoaches, under the motto 'I love my job'. It is the ideal place to exchange experiences, stay up to date with all the latest news, and of course to share successful real-world experiences in career management via LinkedIn. Become a member via the link:
http://www.linkedin.com/e/vgh/2186135